EXPANDING READING SKILLS: INTERMEDIATE 2

SECOND EDITION

Linda Markstein

The Borough of Manhattan Community College
The City University of New York
New York, New York

Louise Hirasawa

The University of Washington
Seattle, Washington

HEINLE & HEINLE PUBLISHERS

A Division of Wadsworth, Inc.
Boston, Massachusetts 02116

Publisher: Stanley J. Galek
Editor: Erik Gundersen
Associate Editor: Lynne Telson Barsky
Editorial Production Manager: Elizabeth Holthaus
Production Editor: Kristin M. Thalheimer
Photo Coordinator: Martha Leibs-Heckly
Manufacturing Coordinator: Jerry Christopher
Project Manager: Anita Raducanu/A+ Publishing Services
Interior Design: Barbara Goodchild
Cover Illustration: Karen Watson
Cover Design: Hannus Design Associates

Heinle & Heinle Publishers is a division of Wadsworth, Inc.

Manufactured in the United States of America

Photograph and Text/Realia Credits appear on p. 203, which constitutes a part
of this copyright page.

Library of Congress Cataloging in Publication Data

Markstein, Linda.
    Expanding reading skills, intermediate 2 / Linda Markstein, Louise Hirasawa.--2nd ed.
        p.   cm.
    Rev. ed. of: Expanding reading skills, intermediate. 1982.
    ISBN (invalid) 083842644
    1. English language--Textbooks for foreign speakers.
    2. Readers--1950– I. Hirasawa, Louise. II. Markstein, Linda.
    Expanding reading skills, intermediate. III. Title.
    PE1128.M346 1993
    428.6'4--dc20   92-2700
                                                CIP

ISBN: 0-8384-2644-1

10 9 8 7 6 5 4 3 2 1

CONTENTS

INTRODUCTION

Expanding Reading Skills: Intermediate, Second Edition, is a completely new book. This thoroughly revised program reflects a different orientation toward reading because our philosophy of the nature of reading and our perception of the real reading needs of students have evolved over the years. The new text is based upon an interactive, process model of reading, and it follows the organizational scheme of *Expanding Reading Skills: Advanced,* Second Edition (1990).

Expanding Reading Skills: Intermediate is intended for college students or other adults who want to develop their reading skills for academic, personal, and/or career purposes. The text is also appropriate for high school students. This book was designed for English as a Second Language and English as a Foreign Language students in both academic and nonacademic settings; however, it can be successfully used with native speaking adults in developmental reading classes as well.

Expanding Reading Skills: Intermediate is the third in a five-book reading program designed to meet the needs of students from the beginning through the advanced levels. The program is designed as follows:

- *Developing Reading Skills,* Beginning
- *Developing Reading Skills,* Intermediate 1
- *Expanding Reading Skills,* Intermediate 2
- *Developing Reading Skills,* Advanced 1
- *Expanding Reading Skills,* Advanced 2

This comprehensively revised edition of *Expanding Reading Skills: Intermediate* is composed of five thematic units and a research and writing skills unit:

- **Fashion and Style**
- **Disaster Strikes**
- **Across Many Cultures**
- **Technology: Some Interesting Effects On Our Lives**
- **How to Improve Your Memory**
- **Developing Research and Writing Skills**

Each thematic unit has three or four readings and a variety of reading, writing, discussion, and structure exercises designed to help learners develop comprehension and integrate new ideas with their knowledge and experience of the world. The readings are on challenging and relevant topics and have been selected from a wide variety of published and unpublished sources, including student writing. Students and teachers at the Borough of Manhattan Community College, City University of New York, helped us select the unit themes, and they generously offered us feedback on the materials in the experimental stage. The materials were tested and revised before publication.

Some of the major features of *Expanding Reading Skills: Intermediate,* Second Edition, are:

- ◆ **Extensive prereading activities**: Before they begin reading, learners work together in guided discussion to activate their awareness of the topic. The prereading activities (1) introduce the text in the context of what is already known by the learners, (2) promote a sharing of information by members of the group, (3) encourage speculation on textual content and, finally, (4) set the stage for the learners' successful integration of new ideas and concepts in the text with their knowledge and experience of the world. We recommend that students working together in small groups choose two or three questions to discuss in detail and that a spokesperson from each group later summarize the main points of the group discussion for the whole class.

- ◆ **Thematic organization**: Each of the five units has three or four readings centered on a common theme. The thematic approach allows for a natural recycling and spiraling of concepts, vocabulary, and syntactic structures. The result is that learners develop their reading, thinking, and writing skills more quickly and are highly motivated to expand their efforts as they successfully cope with more and more challenging material. Finally, we have carefully selected the thematic readings so that the learners will be exposed to a variety of content demands and text densities.

- ◆ **Solid reading-writing connection**: Students write about what they read. They explore their own ideas and feelings about each selection in writing, and they read their writing to their classmates. Furthermore, in the expansion section at the end of every unit, students have the opportunity to develop their writing and research skills through a multi-step process approach. They learn how to develop and elaborate their ideas in writing and how to continue the thematic spiral through their own independent research if they wish. The process writing and research section has been placed at the end of the book so students may refer to it as a resource handbook as needed.

- ◆ **Process approach to reading and writing**: Learners are shown how to interact with text in a logical, systematic manner and how to vary their reading approach to suit their reading purpose, and the content and text density demands of the reading. In addition, they learn to alter their reading speed. They learn how to use text features — headings, different print sizes and types — as pointers to meaning and to use context clues to figure out meanings of new words and phrases. They are guided in how to relate their prior knowledge and experience to the text. Finally, they learn that systematic rereading is as important to reading as systematic rewriting is to writing.

◆ **Glossary**: A glossary, with definitions and example sentences, has been added at the end of the text as a quick reference. Students will still need to use their own dictionaries for examining the range of meanings of a word and for words not included in the glossary.

How to Use the Text

We recommend that instructions within the units be followed as closely as possible. For example, every unit begins with an extensive headnote to provide contextual orientation. This headnote helps learners get their bearings before they begin reading by providing useful social and historical information about the topic. This is helpful for all readers, but is particularly useful for students at the intermediate level. Prereading discussion activities follow. We emphasize the importance of giving careful attention to these activities (as outlined above) because they help the learners relate the text to their previous knowledge and experience. Furthermore, the prereading activities promote cooperative learning and encourage a sharing of social and cultural information. In brief, although it is not necessary for all students to discuss all the prereading questions in detail (small groups can choose two or three to examine), the more attention given to the prereading activities, the more successfully the learners will be able to interact with the text.

In the first unit, we recommend that the teacher work directly with the students in helping them recognize the significance of textual features, e.g. headings, subheadings, different prints — and how these features point to meaning and are essential to effective skimming and scanning.

We believe that reading speed is important. However, we have not recommended specific reading times because, in the testing stage, we found that different individuals had significantly different reading abilities and could read and comprehend at varying rates. We encourage teachers to evaluate the reading abilities of their students and help students set reading times that are challenging, yet not frustrating. We note that ESL and EFL students must be consistently encouraged to break the word-by-word reading habit, which in fact interferes with comprehension. Particularly in the beginning, it is important to emphasize to students that they can understand a reading selection even though they do not understand every word.

The second reading of the passage is designed to give the students time to go back over difficult passages of text and to look up words in their glossaries or dictionaries if they wish. We do not encourage students to look up every unfamiliar word and, in the experimental testing, we noted that very few students attempted to do so. Generally, students chose to confer with each other on the meanings of certain words and to look up other words, or words they were still unsure of, on their own.

The third reading is designed to help students integrate old and new concepts and vocabulary found in the text. It is important to encourage students to recognize the purposes and benefits of rereading because many students are not familiar with a process approach to reading and, in fact, may consider rereading a sign of poor reading skills without careful instruction in this area. In certain cases of densely packed text, we have recommended more than three readings.

We recognize that the level of the readings in this book is challenging. Reading is developmental: we learn to read by reading; we learn to read difficult material only by reading difficult material. Finally, we believe that learners at the intermediate level must meet new reading challenges if they are to reach their personal, professional, and vocational goals in the future.

Linda Markstein
New York, New York

Louise Hirasawa
Seattle, Washington

ACKNOWLEDGMENTS

Many people have helped us along the way in the writing and production of this book. We would like to thank Dorien Grunbaum, Anne Habiby, Danielle Kaplan, Suzanna Markstein, Dorothy Seevers, Madavi Rajguru and Cris Townley for assistance they provided with content. Our developmental reviewer, Linda Lee, gave us valuable suggestions for revision. At Heinle & Heinle, we have had the good fortune to have the encouragement and support of a knowledgeable and enthusiastic team: Erik Gundersen, our editor; Lynne Telson Barsky, associate editor; Kristin Thalheimer, production editor; Anita L. Raducanu, project manager; and Martha Leibs-Heckly, photo coordinator. We express our deep gratitude for the generous comments and suggestions made by the many teachers and students at Borough of Manhattan Community College who tested out various units for us — with particular thanks to Paulette Plonchak and Elizabeth Upton. And finally, we must thank, as always, Allan Kent Dart, Barbara Gonzales, Janis Jones and, especially, our patient and loyal husbands, Katsushige Hirasawa and Steve Markstein, for their unflagging support and encouragement. Without these people, this book would not have been possible.

EXPANDING READING SKILLS: INTERMEDIATE 2

Fashion and Style

"People today, especially young people, are obsessed with fashion and style. They care more about what they wear than what they think or believe." You have probably heard this statement many times; maybe you've even thought or said it yourself. But what about in the past? Did people think much about such things then? In this unit, you will read a bit about the history of fashion and style. Warning: be prepared! What you read may surprise you.

Discussion

Before you begin reading, think about the following questions and discuss your answers. *Note:* You may wish to choose two or three questions to explore in detail with a small group of students from your class.

1. Make a list of some of the latest fashions and styles (for example, clothing and hairstyles) in your country. (See p. 159 for list-making suggestions.)

2. Do young people and older people wear the same clothing styles in your country? Please provide information for each group.

CLOTHING STYLES IN MY COUNTRY

Young People	Older People
mini skirts	*suits and ties*

---

3. What are the most popular hairstyles for young people in your country? Bring in pictures of clothing and hairstyles from your country if possible.

4. Can you think of styles among young people that older people dis-
    approve of? What are some of these styles? Why do you think older
    people disapprove? What is your opinion? How do you explain this
    generation gap?
5. Do you approve of people dyeing or bleaching their hair? Shaving
    their heads? Men wearing long hair? Explain.
6. Do you think women are more interested in fashion and style than
    men are? Explain.

C H A P T E R   O N E

Father and Son

Fathers and sons have a long history of disagreeing on many subjects, particularly when the sons are teenagers. The fathers may object to hair: they may think it's too long — or too short. In the dialogue below, a father and son have a disagreement over jewelry — over "just one little earring," of all things!

1.1
First Reading

Read this selection quickly for the main ideas. Look for differences in point of view among the father, the son, and the grandmother. Do *not* stop to look up words in your dictionary.

1 Father: For the last time, you *cannot* have your ears pierced. I don't want to talk about it anymore.

2 Son: But, Dad, all the other guys...

3 Father: I don't care about "all the other guys." I don't care what they do or don't do. That's up to them and their parents. I care about you. And you cannot have your ears pierced, and that's it. It's final. The subject is closed. Now go do your homework.

4 Son: But, Dad, I just want to have *one* ear pierced. One little hole, just one tiny little hole!

5 Father: That's the most ridiculous thing I have ever heard of! Piercing just one ear! That's crazy! People will say you're crazy! One ear pierced! I think you've lost your mind.

6 Son: It's not crazy. It's the style, Dad. All the guys have just one ear pierced. That's the way it's done. It's cool, Dad. Sometimes they have three or four holes in one ear — but in just one ear. It looks great! I want to be in style. I want to be like the other guys.

7   Father: I don't want to talk about this subject anymore. Just forget it — and go do your homework. If you spent as much time thinking about algebra as you do about earrings, you would be at the top of your class.

(The grandmother walks in.)

8   Grandmother: What's going on? I could hear you outside.

9   Father: I'll tell you what's going on — and then maybe you can talk to your grandson and talk some sense, some reason, into him. He wants to have his ears pierced. I mean, he wants to have *one* ear pierced. Have you ever heard of anything so ridiculous?

10   Grandmother: Well...

11   Son: Grandma, all the guys are doing it. It looks great! It's the style. I'm the only guy in my class...

12   Father: That's not true! I am sure you are not the only boy in your class who doesn't have his ears, ear, pierced. But if you are, I'm glad! I would be very proud if you were the only boy who didn't have his ears, ear, pierced!

13   Grandmother: Now, wait a minute, just a minute. I don't see anything wrong with it. It *is* the style. I have noticed lots of boys with their ears pierced. Who is that singer, the one we saw on television last night, that nice-looking...

14   Father: What are you saying? Mom, why are you doing this? Why are you encouraging Nick in this crazy idea, this nonsense?

15   Grandmother: I don't think it's crazy. I don't see anything wrong with it. It's just the style. All the boys are doing it. And, just remember when you were Nick's age, you had long hair. You had a ponytail almost down to your waist!

16   Father: That was different. And, besides, it was not that long. It was — just down to my shoulders.

17 Grandmother: No, it was much longer than your shoulders. But it was the style. All the boys your age had long hair then. Remember? You could hardly tell the boys from the girls.

18 Son: Yeah, Dad, Grandma's right! I remember those old pictures of you with that long hair. And you had a beard too! Remember?

19 Father: The beard was later. But this is different. It's not the same thing.

20 Grandmother: It *is* the same thing. You had long hair. Now the kids have their ears pierced. It's the same thing. It's the style, the fashion. And that's all it is. It's just part of being young, part of growing up, being one of the crowd...

21 Father: Well, I don't know. I don't like the idea of Nick with a pierced ear, a *hole* in his ear...

22 Grandmother: I didn't like the idea of your long hair at the time. I *hated* that ponytail! And so did your father. But you liked it. And it didn't hurt you. You turned out all right, don't you think?

23 Father: Well...

24 Son: So, what do you think, Dad? Can I do it?

25 Father: Well...I'll think it over. Meanwhile, get back to your algebra...

Reading Times	**Reading Speed**
1st reading _____ minutes	5 minutes = 128 words per minute
3rd reading _____ minutes	4 minutes = 160 wpm
	3 minutes = 213 wpm
	2 minutes = 320 wpm

1.2
Second Reading

Go back and read the selection again. Take as much time as you need. Look up some of the unfamiliar words in the glossary at the end of this book or in your dictionary if you wish.

1.3
Third Reading

Read the selection quickly a third time. Concentrate on understanding the main ideas and the meanings of new vocabulary words in the context in which they appear.

1.4
Reader Response

You, the reader, are part of the reading process. Your ideas and your reactions to what you read are important and valuable because the meaning of the reading depends in part on you and the knowledge and experience that you bring to the reading. In order to explore your response to this reading, take out a pen or pencil and a piece of paper and write for 15 minutes about anything that interested you in this selection. You may wish to write about a personal experience this piece reminded you of — or you may wish to agree or disagree with something in the piece. Try to explore *your own thoughts and feelings* as much as possible. Do *not* merely summarize or restate the ideas in this selection. For sample reader responses, turn to page 29. *Note:* These are authentic writings by real students, and we thank these students for permission to use them.

1.5
Response Sharing

Read your response to two or three other people in your class. Listen carefully to what the others have written. After you have discussed each other's responses, talk about other points of interest in the selection.

1.6
Identifying Main Ideas

Working with the same small group, make a list of the main ideas in this selection. Be sure to state the main ideas in your own words. Don't just copy sentences directly from the text. Think carefully about what the writer is trying to tell you.

Example:

People disagree about style and fashion, especially young people and their parents.

1.7
Analyzing the Text

Work with your group members on this exercise. Discuss the answers carefully, particularly if there are disagreements among members of your group. In some cases, there may be more than one possible interpretation.

1. How does the father feel about his son, Nick, getting his ear pierced?

   (a.) He disapproves; he is not in favor of it.

   b. He approves; he wants his son to be in style.

   c. He is indifferent; he doesn't care one way or the other.

   How do you know? Give examples to explain your answer.

2. The grandmother (the father's mother, in this case):

   a. sides with Nick; in other words, she agrees with Nick and supports him.

   b. sides with her son, Nick's father, because she thinks boys should not pierce their ears.

   c. does not have an opinion on whether Nick should have his ear pierced.

   Explain your answer. Give examples from the text.

3. Why does Nick want to have his ear pierced?

4. The grandmother reminds Nick's father that he

   a. had one ear pierced when he was Nick's age.

   b. had long hair when he was Nick's age.

   c. did not study algebra as much as he should have when he was Nick's age.

   Why does she do this? What point is she making?

5. From this passage, we can see that people of different generations (grandparents, parents, and children)

   a. have the same ideas about fashion and style.

   b. have different ideas about fashion and style.

   c. don't care about fashion and style.

1.8
Vocabulary Study

It is important to learn how to figure out word and phrase meanings from the context in which they appear. First, study the italicized words and phrases in their contexts and guess their meanings. Write your guess on the first line. Then, look up the word or phrase in your dictionary and write the definition on the second line.

Example:

(paragraph 3) I don't care about "all the other *guys.*" I don't care what they do or don't do.

a. (guess) ___*all the other boys (men)*___

b. (dictionary) ___*boys, men*___

1. (paragraph 3) That's it. It's final. The subject is *closed*.

a. (guess) _____

b. (dictionary) _____

2. (paragraph 6) I want to be *in style.*

a. (guess) _____

b. (dictionary) _____

3. (paragraph 9) I mean, he wants to have one ear pierced. Have you ever heard of anything so *ridiculous*?

a. (guess) _____

b. (dictionary) _____

4. (paragraph 17) You could *hardly* tell the boys from the girls.

a. (guess) _____

b. (dictionary) _____

5. (paragraph 18) I remember those old pictures of you with that long hair. And you had a *beard* too!

    a. (guess) _____

    b. (dictionary) _____

1.9
Cloze Exercise

Choose the correct word for each blank. Discuss your choices with your group.

What _____*does*_____ it mean when a man
    (1) do – does – did

_____*wears*_____ an earring in his left ear? Abigail Van Buren
(2) wears – wear – wore

(the writer of the "Dear Abby" newspaper advice column) wrote in a

recent column that she _____ know what, if
    (3) doesn't – don't – didn't

anything, this custom meant. Abby _____ flooded
    (4) is – was – will be

with letters after that. Readers around _____
    (5) a – an – the – this – that

world wrote in to explain. One person wrote a letter stating that it

means that the man is gay* and he was _____
    (6) surprise – surprised

that Abby didn't know that. _____
    (7) Another – The other – The

person wrote that it means that the person is a Buddhist**. Another

person _____ that it meant that a sailor
    (8) insist – insists – insisted

had _____ the equator. A woman
    (9) cross – crossed – crossing

_____ from Hong Kong explained that it is
(10) writes – write – writing

_____

gay – homosexual (being physically and emotionally attracted to members of one's own sex)

****a Buddhist** – a follower of Buddhism, an Eastern religion.

protection against bad luck. A historian explained that men have

_____ earrings for centuries (Shakespeare,
<u>(11) wear – wore – worn</u>

Rembrandt, and King James II, for example) in cultures around the

world and that men have actually worn earrings much longer than

women _____. A college student said that he
<u>(12) has – have – had</u>

_____ an earring in his left ear because he is
<u>(13) wears – wear – wore – worn</u>

right-handed and it is easier to put on an earring in his left ear. The

many _____ Abby received to her question prove
<u>(14) response – responses</u>

only one thing clearly: men wear one earring in their left ear because

they want to. _____ as simple as that!
<u>(15) It – Its – It's</u>

1.10
Application, Critical Evaluation, and Synthesis

1. Did you ever have a disagreement with a parent (or your children, if you have children) over fashion and style? What was the disagreement? Please explain.

2. Styles and fashions change. Give examples of some styles and fashions that have changed in the last few years. (You may wish to work on a list of changes with a few other students. See page 157 for brainstorming suggestions.)

3. Do you think parents should tell their teenage children how they should wear their hair and what kind of clothing they should wear? Who should make these decisions? At what point should a person make his or her own decisions about these matters?

4. Do you think school administrators have the right to tell students how they should dress at school? Do students have the right to wear whatever they want to school? Do you think students should wear uniforms to school? Please explain your answers and give examples. Use this chart as a starting point to help you organize your thinking on this subject.

WEARING UNIFORMS	
Advantages	**Disadvantages**

5. What would you say if
   ◆ your son wanted to pierce his ear?
   ◆ your daughter dyed her hair green?
   ◆ your mother dyed her hair to cover up the gray hair? your father dyed his hair?
   ◆ your brother, boyfriend, or husband grew a beard or a mustache?
   ◆ your sister shaved her head and painted designs on her skull?
   ◆ someone in your family told you that you could not cut your hair in a certain way?

C H A P T E R   T W O

Fashion and Style Around the World

In this selection, you will learn a little about the history of fashion and style around the world. Fashions and styles change, but the desire to be fashionable has always been marked in both men and women from the beginning of recorded history.

2.1
First Reading

Read this selection quickly for the main ideas. Pay close attention to the headings. Do *not* stop to look up words in your dictionary.

1   In most countries around the world, fashion and style are important industries. Americans alone spend more than five billion dollars ($5,000,000,000) a year just on hairstyling products, cosmetics, and toiletries (for example, shampoo and soap). This does not include the huge amount of money they spend on clothing so, as we can easily see, fashion does not come cheap. It costs money, a lot of money, to be fashionable. And people are willing to spend that money.

2   Americans are certainly not the only people interested in fashion and style. The French have always been considered very fashionable and stylish, and many of the most important fashion designers — Christian Dior, Chanel, Yves Saint Laurent — have been French. The Italians and the Spanish have their own claims to fashion fame: Giorgio Armani, Cristobel Balenciaga, Caroline Herrara, to name only a few.

3   And fashion goes far beyond the western world. The streets of Tokyo are full of fashionable Japanese women and men. Go to Africa — to Kenya, to Morocco, to Egypt, — it doesn't matter. Go to Central and South America — to Mexico, to Brazil, to Argentina — wherever you go, you will find that fashions and styles are different. But wherever you go, you will also find that fashion and style are important. People spend a lot of time (and money) figuring out how to wear their hair and what kind of clothing, makeup, and jewelry to wear.

The History of Fashion and Style

4   It has been said that people, especially young people, are obsessed with fashion and style in the modern world. This may well be true. But obsession with fashion and style goes back thousands and thousands of years and has never been limited just to young people.

Makeup in Ancient Egypt

5   Let's take a look at ancient Egypt. In 4000 B.C. (six thousand years ago!), there were many beauty shops and perfume factories in Egypt, and makeup was already widely used by both men and women. In fact, archeologists have found evidence of cosmetics (face powder and eye paint) going back at least eight thousand years. Egyptian men and women outlined their eyes with a black substance called kohl, and they wore eye shadow, usually green in color. They altered the shape of their eyebrows with kohl pencils. At that time, the preferred style was to have the eyebrows meet above the nose, so many people drew a line with their kohl pencils to connect their eyebrows in a fashionable straight line.

6   Vanity was so important to Egyptians that it did not even end with life. When Egyptian kings and queens died, their tombs were filled with a large assortment of cosmetics and beauty products, presumably for use in the afterlife. When King Tutankhamen's tomb was opened in the 1920s, among other things, small jars of skin cream, lip color, and rouge were discovered perfectly preserved — still fragrant and ready for use after roughly 3,360 years.

Cosmetics in Ancient Greece and Rome

7   The Greeks and Romans learned about makeup from the Egyptians. The ancient Greeks, however, preferred a natural

appearance. The Greek ideal of beauty and style was a rugged, masculine look and, as a consequence, most Greek men and women did not use cosmetics. Greek courtesans (mistresses of wealthy Greek men) were heavy users of cosmetics, however; they painted their faces, wore perfume, and had their hair styled in elaborate fashions. They even lightened their hair with a mixture of yellow flower petals, bee pollen, and potassium salt because blond hair was considered to be more desirable than dark hair at that time. In Greek culture, it signified purity and innocence, and nobility of mind and action. Not surprisingly, then, many of the great Greek heroes — Achilles and Paris, for example, are described as having light hair.

8 Although most Greeks (with the exception of courtesans) did not use cosmetics or wear makeup, Greek men did try to lighten their hair color in various ways. In the fourth century B.C., a Greek writer named Menander wrote: "The sun's rays are the best means for lightening the hair, as our men well know. After washing their hair with a special ointment made here in Athens, they sit bareheaded in the sun by the hour, waiting for their hair to turn a beautiful golden blond. And it does." It has been suggested that Greek men may have played up the healthy, natural look ever so slightly by a small touch of rouge from time to time.

9 The Greeks may have preferred a natural look, but the Romans certainly did not. In fact, the more makeup and cosmetics, the better in Roman society, and both Roman men and women painted and perfumed themselves heavily. Even soldiers wore makeup and perfume, and they dyed their hair dark. The Romans, unlike the Greeks, preferred dark hair to blond and, with the help of a little dye, most Romans were able to have fashionably dark hair. What was the dye made of? Walnut shells and wild onions. To prevent graying, men were advised to prepare a paste of earthworms and herbs and wear it overnight. There were other popular remedies for baldness, a highly undesirable condition in that world.

10 Other societies had their own unique hair color preferences. From drawings, it appears that early Saxon men dyed their hair and beards blue, red, green, or orange. The Gauls, on the other hand, were committed to red. And in England, during the reign of Elizabeth I, carrot-red hair was the height of fashion. An ambassador to Elizabeth's court once commented slyly that her hair was "of a light never made by nature."

Nail Polish in Ancient China and Egypt

11 Fingernail paint, or nail polish as we would call it today, probably originated in China sometime before 3000 B.C. (five thousand years ago). The color of one's nail polish was related to social position. During the Chou dynasty (600 B.C.) in China, only members of the royal family could wear gold and silver polish. Later, the royal colors changed to red and black. Well-manicured nails were a symbol of culture and high social position. They distinguished aristocrats, who never had to work with their hands, from the working class, who did have to work with their hands.

12 In Egypt also, nail color was connected to social position. Aristocrats at the top of the order wore shades of red: Queen Nefertiti had her fingernails and toenails painted ruby red, and Cleopatra preferred a deep rust red. People of lower rank were not allowed to wear bright nail colors. The brighter the nail color, the higher the social status. The paler the nail color, the lower the social status.

13 Both men and women wore nail polish in the ancient world. As a matter of fact, high-ranking soldiers in Egypt, Babylonia, and Rome spent hours before a battle putting on makeup and having their hair curled and nails painted. This seems odd to us today. Times — and styles — have obviously changed. But that is an important characteristic of style: it is always changing. What is fashionable and stylish one day seems old-fashioned and even weird the next.

14 It has been said that we do not have a single beauty aid or cosmetic today that was not present in some form in the ancient world. For thousands and thousands of years, people have tried in various ways and by various means to make themselves more beautiful. They have spent a lot of time, money, and energy trying to be fashionable and stylish. So, as we can see, our obsession with fashion and style today is nothing new. We are just acting like people have always acted.

Reading Times	**Reading Speed**
1st reading _____ minutes	8 minutes = 153 words per minute
3rd reading _____ minutes	7 minutes = 176 wpm
	6 minutes = 205 wpm
	5 minutes = 246 wpm

2.2
Second Reading

Go back and read the selection again. Take as much time as you need. Look up some of the unfamiliar words in the glossary at the end of this book or in your dictionary if you wish.

2.3
Third Reading

Read the selection quickly a third time. Concentrate on understanding the main ideas and the meanings of new vocabulary words in the context in which they appear.

2.4
Reader Response

In order to explore your response to this reading, write for 15 minutes about anything that interested you in this passage. You may wish to write about a personal experience this piece reminded you of — or you may wish to agree or disagree with something in the piece. Try to explore *your own thoughts and feelings* as much as possible. Do *not* merely summarize or restate the ideas in the selection.

2.5
Response Sharing

Read your response to two or three other people in your class. Listen carefully to what the others have written. After you have discussed each other's responses, talk about other points of interest in the passage.

2.6
Identifying Main Ideas

Working with the same small group, make a list of the main ideas in this selection. Be sure to state the main ideas in your own words. Don't just copy sentences directly from the text. Think carefully about what the writer is trying to tell you.

2.7
Analyzing the Text

Work with your group members on this exercise. Discuss the answers carefully, particularly if there are disagreements among members of your group. In some cases, there may be more than one possible interpretation.

1. According to this passage, makeup and cosmetics

    a. began in the twentieth century.

    b. were heavily used in the ancient world.

    c. have always been used only by women.

2. Some of these statements are true, and some of them are not true. Read each statement carefully and write **T** (true) or **F** (false) in the space.

    a. _T_ The Chinese probably invented nail polish.

    b. _____ In Egypt, commoners (working-class people) wore bright nail polish colors, and the aristocrats wore softer, lighter colors.

    c. _____ The Greeks were not as interested in makeup and cosmetics as the Egyptians and Romans were.

    d. _____ High-ranking Roman soldiers wore nail polish and makeup.

    e. _____ Greeks preferred dark hair to blond hair, and they used to dye their hair to make it darker.

3. Match these numbers. Write in the letter on the left in the appropriate blank.

    a. 2000 B.C.   _a_ about 4,000 years ago

    b. 4000 B.C.   _____ about 1,000 years from now

    c. 1000 A.D.   _____ about 1,000 years ago

    d. 1500 A.D.   _____ about 6,000 years ago

    e. 3000 A.D.   _____ about 500 years ago

4. Cross out the word that is **not** like the other two words. You may look up words in the glossary or in your dictionary.

   a. ancient – old – modern

   b. fashionable – intelligent – stylish

   c. beauty shop – clothing store – barber shop

   d. long hair – blond hair – dark hair

   e. social status – cosmetics – social position

5. Compare ancient Greece and Rome. What were some differences in fashion and style in these cultures?

2.8
Vocabulary Study

Study the italicized words and phrases in their contexts and guess at their meanings. Write your guess on the first line. Then, look up the word or phrase in your dictionary and write the definition on the second line.

1. (paragraph 6) *Vanity* was so important to Egyptians that it did not even end with life. When Egyptian kings and queens died, their tombs were filled with a large assortment of cosmetics and beauty products, presumably for use in the afterlife.

   a. (guess) _____

   b. (dictionary) _____

2. (paragraph 7) The ancient Greeks, however, preferred a natural appearance. The Greek ideal of beauty and style was a *rugged*, masculine look and, as a consequence, most Greek men and women did not use cosmetics.

   a. (guess) _____

   b. (dictionary) _____

3. (paragraph 7) In Greek culture, [blond hair] *signified* purity and innocence, and nobility of mind and action.

   a. (guess) _____

   b. (dictionary) _____

4. and 5. (paragraph 12) People of lower *rank* were not allowed to wear bright nail colors. The brighter the nail color, the higher the social *status*. The paler the nail color, the lower the social *status*.

rank

a. (guess) _____

b. (dictionary) _____

status

a. (guess) _____

b. (dictionary) _____

2.9
Cloze Exercise

Choose the correct word for each blank. Discuss your choices with your group.

Do you know why men button _____ clothes
(1) his – theirs – their

from right to left and women button _____ from left to
(2) their – theirs

right? People _____ are experts in the
(3) who – which – whom – that

history of fashion _____ this custom goes back
(4) say – says – said

to the _____ century at least, according
(5) fifteen – fifteenth

_____ pictures and drawings from
(6) for – with – from – to

_____ periods in the past.
(7) different – differents – difference

_____ fashion experts say that men buttoned their
(8) This – That – These

clothing _____ right to left because they often
(9) to – at – on – in – from

had to dress _____ when they were away
(10) himself – themself – themselves

from home traveling or fighting in wars. Most people _____
(11) are – is

right-handed so it was easier for men to button their clothing from right

to left. Women, however, usually _____ maids to
(12) has – have – had

help them dress. The maids faced the _____ as they
(13) woman – women

helped them dress and buttoned their clothing from right to left. Because

the maids _____ facing the women (and usually
(14) was – were – is – are

right-handed) this meant that the buttons and buttonholes had to be on

the opposite side from the _____.
(15) mens – men's

2.10
Application, Critical Evaluation, and Synthesis

1. Make a list of some of the things that surprised you as you read this chapter. (See page 159 for list-making suggestions.) Explain why they surprised you.

2. In the 1960s, many young men and women around the world, especially in Europe and the United States, had long hair. Some people objected to men having long hair. Why do you think they objected? How do you feel about men having long hair? Or women having very short hair, crewcuts, or shaved heads? Why?

3. Give some examples of fashions and styles that have changed. Compare fashions and styles of 20 or 30 years ago with fashions and styles of today. How are they different?

4. Discuss a fashion or style that you do not like. Why don't you like it?

5. Some people think that teachers and professors should be required to dress in a special way, for example, to wear suits and conservative clothing. They believe that students would respect them more and try to follow their example. Other people believe that teachers and professors should be free to wear whatever they want and that teaching and learning have nothing to do with what people wear. What is your opinion? Why? Use the chart on the next page to help you explore and organize your ideas on this subject.

REASONS PROFESSORS AND TEACHERS SHOULD

Dress Conservatively   **Dress Any Way They Wish**

C H A P T E R ◆ T H R E E

Blue Jeans: 1860s, San Francisco

Around the world people, especially young people, wear jeans. Where did jeans come from? What is the history of this international style? Charles Panati explains in this excerpt from *Extraordinary Origins of Everyday Things* (New York: HarperCollins Publishers), 1987. Reprinted by permission.

3.1
First Reading

Read this selection quickly for the main ideas. Do *not* stop to look up words in your dictionary.

1   Before jeans were blue, even before they were pants, *jean* was a twilled, cotton cloth, similar to denim, used for making sturdy work clothes. The textile was milled in the Italian town of Genoa, which French weavers called *Genes*, the origin of our word "jeans."

2   The origin of blue jeans, though, is really the story of a seventeen-year-old American immigrant tailor named Levi Strauss. When Strauss arrived in San Francisco during the gold rush of the 1850s, he sold much-needed canvas for tents and covered wagons. An astute observer, he realized that miners went through trousers quickly, so Strauss stitched some of his heavy-duty canvas into overalls. Though heavy and stiff, the pants held up so well that Strauss was in demand as a tailor.

3   In the 1860s, he replaced canvas with denim, a softer fabric milled in Nimes, France. Known in Europe as *serge de Nimes*, in America the textile's name was pronounced "denim." And Strauss discovered that dyeing neutral-colored denim pants indigo blue to minimize soil stains greatly increased their popularity. Cowboys, to achieve a snug fit, put on a pair of Strauss's pants, soaked in a horse-watering trough, then lay in the sun to shrink-dry the material...

4   Blue jeans, strictly utilitarian, first became a fashion item in 1935. That year, an advertisement appeared in *Vogue*. It featured two society women in snug-fitting jeans, and it kicked off a trend named "western chic." The fad was minor compared to the one that erupted out of the designer-jeans competition of the 1970s. The pants once intended for work became the costume of play, creating a multimillion-dollar industry. At the height of the designer-jeans war, Calvin Klein jeans, for instance, despite their high price of fifty dollars (or because of it), were selling at the rate of 250,000 pairs a week.

Reading Times	Reading Speed
1st reading _____ minutes	3 minutes = 100 words per minute
3rd reading _____ minutes	2 minutes = 150 wpm
	1 minutes = 300 wpm

3.2
Second Reading

Go back and read the selection again. Take as much time as you need. Look up some of the unfamiliar words in the glossary at the end of this book or in your dictionary if you wish.

3.3
Third Reading

Read the selection quickly a third time. Concentrate on understanding the main ideas and the meanings of new vocabulary words in the context in which they appear.

3.4
Reader Response

In order to explore your response to this reading, write for 15 minutes about anything that interested you in this selection. You may wish to write about a personal experience this selection reminded you of — or you may wish to agree or disagree with something in the selection. Try to explore *your own thoughts and feelings* as much as possible. Do *not* merely summarize or restate the ideas in the selection.

3.5
Response Sharing

Read your response to two or three other people in your class. Listen carefully to what the others have written. After you have discussed each other's responses, talk about other points of interest in the selection.

3.6
Identifying Main Ideas

Working with the same small group, make a list of the main ideas in this selection. Be sure to state the main ideas in your own words. Don't just copy sentences directly from the text. Think carefully about what the writer is trying to tell you.

3.7
Analyzing the Text

Work with your group members on this exercise. Discuss the answers carefully, particularly if there are disagreements among members of your group. In some cases, there may be more than one possible interpretation.

1. What is the subject of this selection?
    a. Levi Strauss
    b. The history of blue jeans
    c. How jeans are made

2. Levi Strauss made his first jeans for:
    a. working people (cowboys and goldminers) in the San Francisco area.
    b. young people who wanted to be fashionable.
    c. small children.

3. Where did the name "jeans" come from?

4. When did jeans first become fashionable? Why? Explain in detail.

5. What happened to the jeans industry in the 1970s? Did it grow or get smaller? Were there any new developments in the industry? Explain in detail.

Miners on a train leaving a coal mine in Scranton, Pennsylvania

3.8
Vocabulary Study

Study the italicized words and phrases in their contexts and guess at their meanings. Write your guess on the first line. Then, look up the word or phrase in your dictionary and write the definition on the second line.

1. (paragraph 1) Before jeans were blue, even before they were pants, jean was a twilled, cotton cloth...used for making *sturdy* work clothes.

   a. (guess) _____

   b. (dictionary) _____

2. and 3. (paragraph 2) An *astute* observer, [Levi Strauss] realized that miners *went through* trousers quickly.

   astute

   a. (guess) _____

   b. (dictionary) _____

went through (to go through)

a. (guess) _____

b. (dictionary) _____

4. and **5.** (paragraph 4) That year, an advertisement appeared in *Vogue*. It featured two society women in…jeans, and it [started] a *trend* named "western *chic.*"

trend

a. (guess) _____

b. (dictionary) _____

chic

a. (guess) _____

b. (dictionary) _____

3.9
Cloze Exercise

Choose the correct word for each blank. Discuss your choices with your group.

The way you wear _____ hair — long, short,
          (1) you're – you – your

curly, straight — _____ a lot about you and
          (2) say – says – said

_____ your place in your society. Hair
(3) about – of – in – for

_____ political importance, believe it or not! In
(4) has – have – had

the 1960s, for _____, young people — both
          (5) example – examples

female and _____ — started wearing
          (6) men – man – male – males

_____ hair very long, usually to show that they
(7) there – they're – their

were against _____ war in Vietnam and
          (8) a – an – the – this – that

concerned about _____ environment, among

<u>(9) a – an – the – this – that</u>

other things. They wanted to change the world of their parents, and

they _____ by changing their own appearance

<u>(10) start – starts – started</u>

so that they did not look, act, or dress like their parents. Their hair,

long and sometimes wild-looking, was part of their political statement

to the world that they were breaking from the past.

3.10
Application, Critical Evaluation, and Synthesis

1. Do people in your culture wear jeans? Are jeans popular? Among everyone or just people of a certain age? Explain and give examples.
2. Do you have a favorite pair of jeans? If so, describe and explain. What do these jeans mean to you? Why? Start off by making a "jeans" map to explore your ideas and associations (see page 160 for map-making guidance).

3. Do you think people (students and/or teachers) should wear jeans to school? To work? Why? Or why not? Explain your reasons with clear examples.
4. Write about your favorite article of clothing (for example, a special sweater, shirt). Describe this piece of clothing in detail. Where did you get it? When? Why is it important to you? What does it mean to you? How do you feel about yourself when you are wearing it?
5. "You are what you wear." Write a composition using this statement as your main idea. First, do a short freewriting (see p. 161 for instruction on freewriting) to explore your ideas. *Note:* You may wish to follow up your first freewriting with a second one (see p. 162) to develop and clarify your ideas on your subject.

AT THE END OF EVERY UNIT, YOU ARE INVITED TO TURN TO THE EXPANSION SECTION ON PAGE 155. THIS SECTION CONCENTRATES ON SOME OF THE FUNDAMENTALS OF WRITING.

Sample Reader Response #1 See 1.4, page 6

This is an interesting topic for me because the same thing happened in my family. My father got very upset when my older brother pierced his ear when he was in high school. At the time it was very strange for all of us because we had just immigrated and this youth custom was unknown to us. My older brother was becoming Americanized very fast because he was in high school. My father and mother were completely Chinese and followed the old ways. It was a crisis for our family. My brother won.

Sample Reader Response #2

I am not a narrow mind person but still it is a strange idea for me for man to wear earrings. In my culture earrings are only for the woman. All women even small girls wear earrings but I never see a man wearing an earring or earrings. If he does, he will not be accepted as a man I think. But for me, it's alright. I think people can be different, have different ideas. In my culture though there is not very great respect for differences. We don't think about style from an individual point of view. Anyway this is very interesting topic and I like to think more about it.

Disaster Strikes

Nature can be very beautiful, but it can also be dangerous. Newspapers and television often show us terrible floods, hurricanes, typhoons, tornados, windstorms, sandstorms, earthquakes, volcanos, and avalanches. These natural disasters can be frightening. They can cause great damage. Yet we are all fascinated by the powerful forces that cause them. This unit looks at earthquakes — what they are, how they happen, and how they affect our lives.

Discussion

Before you begin reading, think about the following questions and discuss your answers.

1. What do you know about earthquakes? What do the pictures on pages 30, 33, 50, and 55 tell you about earthquakes?
2. Have you ever been in (or read about) an earthquake? What happened? How did you react?
3. Would you live in a city if you knew that it regularly had serious earthquakes? Why?
4. What other kinds of natural disasters do you know about? Have you ever experienced one? Work with your small group to make a chart like the one below. List all the natural disasters you can think of. Then describe what happens when they occur.

NATURAL DISASTERS	
Natural Disaster	**What Happens?**
Volcano	Clouds of steam and rock shoot up into the air.
	Hot lava runs down the side of the mountain.
	Ashes cover the ground.

C H A P T E R   O N E

The Ground Shook, and Then It Shook Again

Between December 1988 and July 1990, there were serious earthquakes in four countries around the world. Why do earthquakes occur? This article describes what earthquakes are and how they happen.

1.1
First Reading

Read this selection quickly for the main ideas. Pay attention to the title and the main ideas as you read. Do *not* stop to look up words in your dictionary.

1   Earthquake! Armenia, Iran, the Philippines, San Francisco (U.S.A.). The ground shook. Then it shook again, and again. The earth moved back and forth, up and down, like waves on the ocean. Buildings swayed and cracked. Houses fell down. Steel beams twisted. People ran out of their houses screaming in terror. In Iran and Armenia, thousands of people were injured or left homeless. Many people died. Roads were closed because of rock and mud slides. It was difficult for rescue workers and trucks with food and supplies to get in. A survivor in Iran said, "I saw the mountain slide toward the village." In San Francisco, a section of a big bridge fell. A double-decker highway collapsed, crushing cars and the people in them. Businesses were damaged or destroyed. People were without electricity, gas, or water.

2   In less than a year and a half, there were major earthquakes in these four countries. The earthquakes lasted 15-30 seconds. But that was just the beginning. For many days, there were "aftershocks" that shook the ground as the earth kept settling. Each aftershock made people nervous. They couldn't sleep. They were afraid to drive or walk over bridges or to go into buildings. They were afraid there would be another big earthquake. They said "When will this ever stop?"

3   Many countries helped the Philippines, Armenia, and Iran. They sent medical supplies, food, and rescue teams. Great Britain and Switzerland sent specialists in earthquake safety design to San Francisco to help evaluate the damage.

4   **How big were these earthquakes?**
These four earthquakes registered from 6.9 to 7.7 on the Richter scale. The Richter scale goes from 1 to 9. It measures how strong an earthquake is. A measurement over 4 on this scale can cause damage. A 7 is very serious. Many of the aftershocks registered from 3 to 5 on this scale.

5   **Can you predict when an earthquake will happen?**
It is impossible to predict exactly when an earthquake will happen, but scientists can estimate where and when one will occur.

6   **How does an earthquake happen?**
Earthquakes happen when two "plates," huge parts of the earth's crust, move suddenly. Scientists believe there are 10 large plates and several smaller ones. They all move a few centimeters a year. When two plates push together for many years or slip against each other, pressure builds up and an earthquake occurs. The longer and harder the plates push, the bigger the earthquake. (If this pressure produces a lot of heat and melts the rock inside the earth, it can cause a volcano to erupt.)

7   **Where do earthquakes occur?**
Earthquakes occur at the edges between two plates, along cracks in the earth called "faults." The fault near San Francisco is called the San Andreas Fault. It is 750 miles long (1250 kilometers). San Francisco had a terrible earthquake along this fault in 1906, another serious one in 1971, and a big one in 1989. The 1971 earthquake raised the height of some nearby mountains by four feet (1.2 meters).

8   San Francisco is on the North American plate. Los Angeles is on a different plate, the Pacific plate. The Los Angeles plate is moving north; the San Francisco plate is moving south. Someday, millions of years from now, Los Angeles and San Francisco will be next to each other. In 1989, the earthquake moved San Francisco 6.5 feet (2 meters) closer to Los Angeles.

9   Earthquakes are common around the edges of the enormous Pacific plate — in China, Japan, Indonesia, the Philippines, western United States, and Mexico. Other areas with frequent earthquakes — Italy, Greece, Iran, and Turkey — are also along the edges of plates.

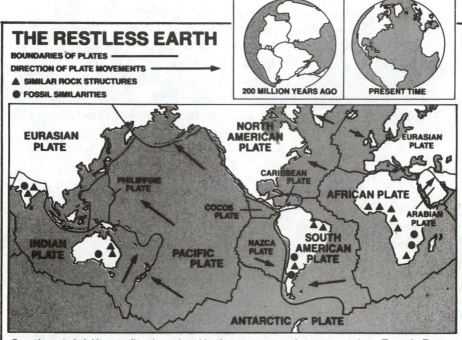

THE RESTLESS EARTH

BOUNDARIES OF PLATES ————
DIRECTION OF PLATE MOVEMENTS ————▶
▲ SIMILAR ROCK STRUCTURES
● FOSSIL SIMILARITIES

200 MILLION YEARS AGO | PRESENT TIME

EURASIAN PLATE

NORTH AMERICAN PLATE

EURASIAN PLATE

PHILIPPINE PLATE

CARIBBEAN PLATE

AFRICAN PLATE

COCOS PLATE

ARABIAN PLATE

INDIAN PLATE

PACIFIC PLATE

NAZCA PLATE

SOUTH AMERICAN PLATE

ANTARCTIC PLATE

Continental drift was first imagined in the seventeenth century, when Francis Bacon observed that the contours of the earth's continents would fit together, like pieces in a puzzle, to form a single continent. The idea was dismissed. Much later, discoveries of similar rocks and fossils along latitudinal lines but on different continents supported the theory that continents and oceans are plates drifting across the earth.

10 **Why do some buildings get damaged while others nearby remain unharmed?**

Earthquakes cause many complex types of movement, both on the surface and deep underground. It is impossible to predict the direction in which an earthquake will shake the ground. The chance of damage depends on the type of construction, on the direction in which the ground moves, and on other factors. Many buildings in Armenia and the highway in San Francisco were destroyed because the soil underneath them was soft and unstable. When water rose into the soil, the structures on them began to "float" and then fell apart.

11 **Will there be another big earthquake in these places?**
Yes, all these areas will have more earthquakes in the future.
Scientists are already predicting that there will be another earthquake in San Francisco sometime within the next 20-30 years,
even bigger than the 1989 quake. How big could it be? Well, an
earthquake in Alaska in 1964 measured 8.5 on the Richter scale.
It raised the earth in some places almost fifty feet (15.3 meters).
The Mexico City earthquake in 1985 measured 8.1. The next
"big one" in San Francisco would likely measure 7 or greater.

Reading Times	Reading Speed
1st reading _____ minutes	9 minutes = 92 wpm
3rd reading _____ minutes	8 minutes = 103 wpm
	7 minutes = 118 wpm
	6 minutes = 138 wpm
	5 minutes = 165 wpm

1.2
Second Reading

Go back and read the selection again. Take as much time as you need.
Look up some of the unfamiliar words in the glossary at the end of this
book or in your dictionary if you wish.

1.3
Third Reading

Read the selection quickly a third time. Concentrate on understanding
the main ideas and the meanings of new vocabulary words in the
context in which they appear.

1.4
Reader Response

In order to explore your response to this reading, write for 15 minutes about anything that interests you in this selection. You may wish to write about a personal experience this reading reminded you of — or about how you feel when you hear about natural disasters. Try to explore *your own thoughts and feelings* as much as possible. Do *not* merely summarize or restate the ideas in the selection.

1.5
Response Sharing

Read your response to two or three other people in your class. Listen carefully to what the others have written. After you have discussed each other's responses, talk about other points of interest in the selection.

1.6
Identifying Main Ideas

Working with the same small group, make a list of the main ideas in this selection. Be sure to state the main ideas in your own words. Don't just copy sentences directly from the text. Think carefully about what the writer is trying to tell you.

1.7
Analyzing the Text

Work with your group members on this exercise. Discuss the answers carefully, particularly if there are disagreements among members of your group. In some cases, there may be more than one possible interpretation.

1. Paragraphs 1, 2, and 3 are very __A__, while paragraphs 4–11 are very __B__. (Choose one phrase for space A and another for space B.)

   a. factual and scientific
   b. descriptive and dramatic
   c. unsympathetic and disinterested

   Find two examples from the reading that explain why you made each choice.

2. Paragraph 2 describes:

    a. the effect of aftershocks.

    b. how long an earthquake lasts.

    c. where major earthquakes occur.

3. In paragraph 6, what are "plates"?

    a. huge parts of the earth's crust

    b. small earthquakes that move suddenly

    c. hot rocks that cause volcanoes to erupt

4. In paragraph 9, Italy, Greece, Iran, and Turkey are between dashes (—) to show that:

    a. they are along the edge of the Pacific plate.

    b. they are the only countries in Europe and the Middle East with frequent earthquakes.

    c. these are examples of other areas with frequent earthquakes.

5. In paragraph 11, why are the Alaska and Mexico City earthquakes described?

    a. They are examples of very large earthquakes that occurred recently in the same part of the world as San Francisco.

    b. They are examples of earthquakes over 8.0 on the Richter scale.

    c. They are areas of the world that people should stay away from if they want to avoid earthquakes.

1.8
Vocabulary Study

Study the italicized words and phrases in their contexts and guess their meanings. Write your guess on the first line. Then, look up the word or phrase in your dictionary and write the definition on the second line.

1. (paragraph 1) The ground *shook*. Then it shook again, and again. The earth moved back and forth, up and down.

    a. (guess) _____

    b. (dictionary) _____

2. (paragraph 1) People ran out of their houses screaming in *terror*.

    a. (guess) _____

    b. (dictionary) _____

3. (paragraph 1) A double-decker highway collapsed, *crushing* cars and the people in them.

    a. (guess) _____

    b. (dictionary) _____

4. (paragraph 5) It is impossible to *predict* exactly when an earthquake will happen, but scientists can estimate where and when one will occur.

    a. (guess) _____

    b. (dictionary) _____

5. (paragraph 10) Why do some buildings get damaged while others nearby remain *unharmed*?

    a. (guess) _____

    b. (dictionary) _____

1.9
Reading Charts

Look at the charts on pages 41 and 42, and answer these questions. Discuss your answers with your small group.

1. Look at Chart 1. This chart shows:
   a. only earthquakes with reliable seismograph measurements.
   b. all earthquakes from the year 526–1990.
   c. major earthquakes from the year 526–1990.

2. What does "Mag." mean?

   a. a tenfold increase in energy
   b. the magnitude of earthquakes on the Richter scale
   c. deaths and damage caused

3. Is the magnitude for the 1755 Portugal earthquake the actual Richter scale measurement?

   a. Yes, it is the actual measurement.
   b. No, it is an estimate.

   How do you know?

4. Which was the worst earthquake on this chart? Why do you think so?

5. Overall, which country has suffered the worst earthquakes? Why do you think so?

6. True or False: The Richter scale measures only the movement of the earth. It does not indicate the number of deaths or the amount of damage.

   What information on the chart tells you the correct answer?

7. Look at Chart 2. Where did the information for this chart come from?

   a. the Richter scale
   b. the countries that had the earthquakes
   c. the Global Volcanism Network

8. Do you think all the earthquakes on Chart 2 are considered "significant"?

   a. Yes
   b. No
   c. I don't know.

   Why do you think so?

Chart 1

Major Earthquakes

Magnitude of earthquakes (Mag.) distinct from deaths or damage caused, is measured on the Richter scale, on which each higher number represents a tenfold increase in energy measured in ground motion. Adopted in 1935, the scale has been applied in the following table to earthquakes as far back as reliable seismograms are available.

Date	Place	Deaths	Mag.
526 May 20	Syria, Antioch	250,000	N.A.
856 —	Greece, Corinth	45,000	"
1057 —	China, Chihli	25,000	"
1268 —	Asia Minor, Cilicia	60,000	"
1290 Sept. 27	China, Chihli	100,000	"
1293 May 20	Japan, Kamakura	30,000	"
1531 Jan. 26	Portugal, Lisbon	30,000	"
1556 Jan. 24	China, Shaanxi	830,000	"
1667 Nov.	Caucasia, Shemaka	80,000	"
1693 Jan. 11	Italy, Catania	60,000	"
1730 Dec. 30	Japan, Hokkaido	137,000	"
1737 Oct. 11	India, Calcutta	300,000	"
1755 June 7	Northern Persia	40,000	"
1755 Nov. 1	Portugal, Lisbon	60,000	8.75*
1783 Feb. 4	Italy, Calabria	30,000	N.A.
1797 Feb. 4	Ecuador, Quito	41,000	"
1811-12	New Madrid, Mo. (series)	—	8.7*
1822 Sept. 5	Asia Minor, Aleppo	22,000	"
1828 Dec. 28	Japan, Echigo	30,000	"
1868 Aug 13-15	Peru and Ecuador	40,000	"
1875 May 16	Venezuela, Colombia	16,000	"
1886 Aug. 31	Charleston, S.C.	60	6.6
1896 June 15	Japan, sea wave	27,120	N.A.
1906 Apr. 18-19	San Francisco, Cal.	503	8.3
1906 Aug. 16	Chile, Valparaiso	20,000	8.6
1908 Dec. 28	Italy, Messina	83,000	7.5
1915 Jan. 13	Italy, Avezzano	29,980	7.5
1920 Dec. 16	China, Gansu	100,000	8.6
1923 Sept. 1	Japan, Yokohama	200,000	8.3
1927 May 22	China, Nan-Shan	200,000	8.3
1932 Dec. 26	China, Gansu	70,000	7.6
1933 Mar. 2	Japan	2,990	8.9
1933 Mar. 10	Long Beach, Cal.	115	6.2
1934 Jan. 15	India, Bihar-Nepal	10,700	8.4
1935 May 31	India, Quetta	50,000	7.5
1939 Jan. 24	Chile, Chillan	28,000	8.3
1939 Dec. 26	Turkey, Erzincan	30,000	7.9
1946 Dec. 21	Japan, Honshu	2,000	8.4
1948 June 28	Japan, Fukui	5,131	7.3
1949 Aug. 5	Ecuador, Pelileo	6,000	6.8
1950 Aug. 15	India, Assam	1,530	8.7
1953 Mar. 18	NW Turkey	1,200	7.2
1956 June 10-17	N. Afghanistan	2,000	7.7
1957 July 2	Northern Iran	2,500	7.4
1957 Dec. 13	Western Iran	2,000	7.1
1960 Feb. 29	Morocco, Agadir	12,000	5.8
1960 May 21-30	Southern Chile	5,000	8.3
1962 Sept. 1	Northwestern Iran	12,230	7.1
1963 July 26	Yugoslavia, Skopje	1,100	6.0
1964 Mar. 27	Alaska	131	8.4
1966 Aug. 19	Eastern Turkey	2,520	6.9
1968 Aug. 31	Northeastern Iran	12,000	7.4
1970 Jan. 5	Yunnan Province, China	10,000	7.7
1970 Mar. 28	Western Turkey	1,086	7.4
1970 May 31	Northern Peru	66,794	7.7
1971 Feb. 9	San Fernando Valley, Cal.	65	6.6
1972 Apr. 10	Southern Iran	5,057	6.9
1972 Dec. 23	Nicaragua	5,000	6.2
1974 Dec. 28	Pakistan (9 towns)	5,200	6.3
1975 Sept. 6	Turkey (Lice, etc.)	2,312	6.7
1976 Feb. 4	Guatemala	22,778	7.5
1976 May 6	Northeast Italy	946	6.5
1976 June 26	New Guinea, Irian Java	443	7.1
1976 July 28	China, Tangshan	242,000	8.2
1976 Aug. 17	Philippines, Mindanao	8,000	7.8
1976 Nov. 24	E. Turkey	4,000	7.9
1977 Mar. 4	Romania	1,541	7.5
1977 Aug. 19	Indonesia	200	8.0
1977 Nov. 23	Northwestern Argentina	100	8.2
1978 June 12	Japan, Sendai	21	7.5
1978 Sept. 16	Northeast Iran	25,000	7.7
1979 Sept. 12	Indonesia	100	8.1
1979 Dec. 12	Colombia, Ecuador	800	7.9
1980 Oct. 10	Northwestern Algeria	4,500	7.3
1980 Nov. 23	Southern Italy	4,800	7.2
1982 Dec. 13	North Yemen	2,800	6.0
1983 Mar. 31	Southern Colombia	250	5.5
1983 May 26	N. Honshu, Japan	81	7.7
1983 Oct. 30	Eastern Turkey	1,300	7.1
1985 Mar. 3	Chile	146	7.8
1985 Sept. 19, 21	Mexico City	4,200+	8.1
1987 Mar. 5-6	NE Ecuador	4,000+	7.3
1988 Aug. 20	India/Nepal border	1,000+	6.5
1988 Nov. 6	China/Burma border	1,000	7.3
1988 Dec. 7	NW Armenia	55,000+	6.8
1989 Oct. 17	San Francisco Bay Area	62	6.9
1990 May 30	N. Peru	115	6.3
1990 June 21	Romania	8	6.5
1990 June 21	N. Iran	40,000+	7.7
1990 July 16	Luzon, Philippines	1,621	7.7
1991 Feb. 1	Pakistan/Afghanistan border	1,220	6.8

(*) estimated from earthquake intensity. (N.A.) not available.

Reprinted by permission of *The World Almanac & Book of Facts, 1991*

Chart 2

Some Recent Earthquakes

Source: Global Volcanism Network, Smithsonian Institution

Attached is a list of recent earthquakes. Magnitude of earthquakes is measured on the Richter scale, on which each higher number represents a tenfold increase in energy measured in ground motion. A quake is considered significant if it has a magnitude of 6.5 on the Richter scale or if it causes casualties or considerable damage.

Date	Place	Magnitude	Date	Place	Magnitude
May 30, 1991	S. Alaska	6.8	Feb. 20	Japan	6.5
May 24	S. Peru	6.8	Feb. 19	Vanuatu	6.8
May 19	Indonesia	6.9	Feb. 19	New Zealand	6.3
Apr. 29	Georgia, U.S.S.R.	7.2	Feb. 8	Philippines	6.6
Apr. 22	Costa Rica, Panama	7.4	Jan. 16	N. California	5.5
Feb. 9	Solomon Islands	6.9	Dec. 30, 1989	Bismarck Sea	6.7
Jan. 5	Burma	7.1	Dec. 27	Australia	5.4
Dec. 30, 1990	New Britain	6.7	Dec. 15	Philippines	7.3
Nov. 15	Indonesia	6.9	Nov. 20	SW China	5.1
Nov. 6	S. Iran	6.8	Nov. 1	Off Japan coast	7.3
Oct. 17	W. Brazil	6.7	Oct. 29	Algeria	5.3
Sept. 2	W. Ecuador	6.1	Oct. 18	NE China	5.3
Aug. 3	NW China	6.1	Oct. 18	San Francisco Bay Area	6.9
July 9	Sudan	6.5	Oct. 7	Aleutian Islands	6.7
June 20	NW Iran	7.7	Sept. 22	W. China	6.2
May 30	N. Peru	6.3	Sept. 4	Indonesia	6.1
May 30	Romania	6.5	Aug. 20	Ethiopia	6.3
Mar. 25	Costa Rica	7.1	May 23	Macquane Island	8.3
Feb. 28	S. California	5.5	Apr. 25	Mexico	6.8

Reprinted by permission of *The World Almanac & Book of Facts,* 1991

1.10
Application, Critical Evaluation, and Synthesis

1. Is there a natural disaster that happens often in your native country? What is it? How often does it happen? How do people prepare for it?

2. Have you ever been in a terrible natural disaster? Was there any warning? What happened? How did you feel? How did people protect themselves? (If you have never been in this situation yourself, have you read about one in a newspaper or magazine?)

3. Using an encyclopedia, look up one other kind of natural disaster (such as a volcano or typhoon). Make a short report on it. Some questions you might want to answer are: Where does it occur? How often does it occur? Is it only at one time of year? How does it happen? What kind of destruction does it cause? Can scientists predict it? (See page 167 on "Encyclopedias" and page 170 on "Taking Notes" in the Expansion section, to help you organize your report.)

C H A P T E R   T W O

Predicting Earthquakes

Is it possible to predict earthquakes right before they happen? Scientists are looking for ways to make accurate predictions of where, when, and how strong an earthquake will be. The information in this reading comes from several *Nova* and *Fire on the Rim* television programs (Public Broadcasting System, 1990) and from articles in *Science Digest*, June 1981, and the *Christian Science Monitor*, December 15, 1990.

2.1
First Reading

Read this article quickly for the main ideas. Pay attention to the title and the main ideas as you read. Do *not* stop to look up words in your dictionary.

1   Are there any clues that could alert people to an upcoming earthquake? Earthquakes are extremely difficult to predict. While scientists know where earthquakes are likely to occur, they have not yet found ways to make short-term predictions. And often, by the time they realize what is going on, it is too late.

2   Earthquakes occur frequently around the Pacific Rim plate. When earthquakes shake the ocean floor, they create great waves, called tsunami, which can be as tall as a building. These huge waves come up onto the shore again and again with terrible force, and then they roll out across the ocean.

3   In 1960, there was a great earthquake in Chile that measured 8.3 on the Richter scale. Three thousand people died. Half of them drowned in an enormous tsunami wave. The wave then rolled on to Hawaii, where it lifted up houses, killed 61 people, and injured hundreds more. It continued on to Japan, 4,000 miles away, where 180 people lost their lives. This tremendous wave had traveled over 11,000 miles in 22 hours, but there was no warning in Hawaii or Japan because the people did not feel the earthquake. This event led to the creation of an international Tsunami Warning Center in Hawaii, which communicates with another major Tsunami Center in Japan by satellites. At these centers, scientists can locate earthquakes anywhere in the Pacific within 12 minutes, determine the direction of the wave, and send a warning to countries all around the Pacific within 20 minutes. While these centers can help people who live far away from the earthquake, they can't help those who live near the epicenter (where the tsunami wave started).

4   Volcanoes are related to earthquakes. Japan has one-tenth of the earth's 800 volcanoes, and many of them are constantly erupting. In Sakurajima in Japan, mudslides, floods and ash regularly damage homes and roads. The biggest danger is burning hot rocks that fly out of the volcano and crash into people's homes and shops. Seven billion yen ($54 million) are spent every year cleaning up after these eruptions. Some scientists in Sakurajima are confident they can predict an eruption four to ten days in advance by watching for an increase in seismic (earthquake) activity on computers and other scientific equipment.

5   Technology can help predict earthquakes and some scientists believe that animals can too. In the Peoples Republic of China, for example, the Chinese use many techniques to predict earthquakes. They look for small changes in the water level in wells. They listen for unusual noises that come from the ground in the days just before an earthquake and sound like gunfire or thunder. They monitor slow changes in electromagnetic currents in the earth and measure the levels of certain gases in water. They monitor small quakes on seismographs. And they also observe strange animal behavior.

6   For centuries, the Chinese have observed that some animals behave in unusual ways right before an earthquake. Roosters crow at the wrong time of day, and chickens and geese fly around excitedly. Dogs bark for no reason. Fish jump wildly. Animals that usually remain hidden, like snakes and rats, suddenly come out into the open. Horses, cows, and pigs — which are usually calm animals — become very restless, and run around anxiously.

7   Why do animals react this way? Animals are far more sensitive to natural phenomena than humans. For example, dogs can hear sound waves much higher than humans. Birds and bees use the earth's magnetic field when they fly. Snakes are highly sensitive to minute vibrations in the earth. Slight changes in any of these phenomena could cause animals to panic, and the Chinese believe that, because of this sensitivity, animals can pick up danger signals long before an earthquake happens. For example, fish could detect early earthquake movement under water, and animals which are sensitive to smell could detect minute amounts of gases released just as an earthquake was beginning.

8   China has a nationwide system that relies on people in small villages to report unusual seismic activity and odd animal behavior. To help them, the government has given out fans with pictures of frightened horses, jumping fish, and chickens in trees. Poems on the fans describe this strange animal behavior and encourage every family to report unusual events. Not all Western scientists believe that animals are reliable predictors of earthquakes, but they are watching the Chinese research closely.

9   While scientists can't tell people for sure exactly when a quake will occur, they can predict well enough to help people prepare. Their work is not easy since earthquakes follow a wide variety of patterns. Some have lots of warnings, others have none. Earthquakes operate on geologic time (hundreds, thousands of years), not human time (a few decades). So the warnings may be there, but just too infrequent for humans to be able to see the patterns in one lifetime. Scientists tend to be conservative in their predictions. They are concerned that if they guess wrong, people will stop believing them — and that could have serious consequences.

Reading Times	Reading Speed
1st reading _____ minutes	10 minutes = 83 wpm
3rd reading _____ minutes	8 minutes = 104 wpm
	7 minutes = 119 wpm
	6 minutes = 140 wpm
	5 minutes = 168 wpm
	4 minutes = 210 wpm

2.2
Second Reading

Go back and read the selection again. Take as much time as you need. Look up some of the unfamiliar words in the glossary at the end of this book or in your dictionary if you wish.

2.3
Third Reading

Read the selection quickly a third time. Concentrate on understanding the main ideas and the meanings of new vocabulary words in the context in which they appear.

2.4
Reader Response

In order to explore your response to this reading, write for 15 minutes about anything that interests you in this selection. You may wish to write about another description of disaster prediction that this reading reminded you of — or you may wish to agree or disagree with something in the reading. Try to explore *your own thoughts and feelings* as much as possible. Do *not* merely summarize or restate the ideas in the selection.

2.5
Response Sharing

Read your response to two or three other people in your class. Listen carefully to what the others have written. After you have discussed each other's responses, talk about other points of interest in the selection.

2.6
Identifying Main Ideas

Working with the same small group, make a list of the main ideas in this selection. Be sure to state the main ideas in your own words. Don't just copy sentences directly from the text. Think carefully about what the writer is trying to tell you.

2.7
Analyzing the Text

Work with your group members on this exercise. Discuss the answers carefully, particularly if there are disagreements among members of your group. In some cases, there may be more than one possible interpretation.

1. Paragraph 1 says "Often by the time scientists realize what is going on, it is too late." Why is it too late?

    a. An earthquake has already happened.

    b. The short-term predictions are wrong.

    c. They don't know when earthquakes are likely to occur.

2. What are *tsunami*? (paragraph 2)

    a. earthquakes on the ocean floor

    b. Pacific Rim plate earthquakes

    c. great waves caused by an underwater earthquake

3. The general topic of paragraph 3 is:

    a. the earthquake in Chile.

    b. tsunami waves.

    c. the number of deaths.

    Please explain your answer.

4. Read paragraphs 6 and 7. Paragraph 6:

    a. is not connected to paragraph 7.

    b. contradicts what paragraph 7 explains.

    c. gives examples of what paragraph 7 explains.

5. "Not all Western scientists believe that animals are reliable predictors of earthquakes...." (paragraph 8). *Not all* means:

    a. no Western scientists believe animals are reliable predictors.

    b. some Western scientists believe animals are reliable predictors.

    c. Western scientists will never believe animals are reliable predictors.

2.8
Vocabulary Study

Study the italicized words and phrases in their contexts and guess their meanings. Write your guess on the first line. Then, look up the word or phrase in your dictionary and write the definition on the second line.

1. (paragraph 4) Many of these volcanoes are constantly *erupting*. In Sakurajima, mudslides, floods, and ash regularly damage homes and roads.

    a. (guess) _____

    b. (dictionary) _____

2. (paragraph 6) Horses, cows, and pigs — which are usually calm animals — become very *restless*, and run around anxiously.

    a. (guess) _____

    b. (dictionary) _____

3. (paragraph 7) Animals which are sensitive to smell could *detect* minute amounts of gases released just as an earthquake was beginning.

    a. (guess) _____

    b. (dictionary) _____

4. (paragraph 9) Earthquakes follow a wide variety of *patterns*. Some have lots of warnings, others have none.

    a. (guess) _____

    b. (dictionary) _____

5. (paragraph 9) Earthquakes operate on geologic time (hundreds, thousands of years), not human time (a few decades). So the warnings may be there, but just too *infrequent* for humans to be able to see the patterns in one lifetime.

   a. (guess) _____

   b. (dictionary) _____

2.9
Special Expressions

The phrases in italics have special meanings. Study these phrases in their contexts. Then choose the definition from the list below that means the same thing and write it over the phrase. Be sure to use correct verb tenses and singular or plural forms for nouns. Check your answers in your glossary or dictionary.

before (something) happens   immediately
definitely   to make (something) clean again
to distribute   to notice
to happen

1. (paragraph 1) Often, by the time scientists realize what *is going on*, it is too late.
2. (paragraph 4) Seven billion yen are spent every year *cleaning up* the city after these eruptions.
3. (paragraph 4) Some scientists in Sakurajima are confident they can predict an eruption four to ten days *in advance*.
4. (paragraph 6) For centuries, the Chinese have observed that some animals behave in unusual ways *right* before an earthquake.
5. (paragraph 7) Animals are far more sensitive to natural phenomena than humans, so they can *pick up* danger signals long before an earthquake happens.
6. (paragraph 8) The government *has given out* fans with pictures of frightened horses, jumping fish, and chickens in trees.
7. (paragraph 9) While scientists can't tell people *for sure* exactly when a quake will occur, they can predict well enough to help people prepare.

2.10
Application, Critical Evaluation, and Synthesis

1. What would be the benefits of predicting earthquakes or volcanic eruptions? Working with your small group, brainstorm some ideas (see page 157 in the Expansion section).

2. If you were the mayor of a city and were told an earthquake would occur in four days, what would you do? What would you tell people to do? What would you tell the police, fire department, hospitals and other public services to do? Outline your ideas (see page 176 in the Expansion section).

3. Think of some other natural disaster (such as a typhoon, flood or volcano). What kind of long range planning would you suggest for people who live in the area? In general, how could a city or town prepare?

4. Paragraph 9 says there could be serious consequences if scientists guess wrong. What do you think some consequences might be? Why could they be serious?

CHAPTER THREE

Glimpses After the Earthquake: San Francisco, 1989

This section is made up of two newspaper articles. They are brief stories of how some people reacted after the San Francisco earthquake in 1989. The earthquake measured 6.9 on the Richter scale. Sixty-two people died; 59 of them were crushed when the upper roadway of the Nimitz Freeway collapsed. The earthquake destroyed buildings mainly in one area of the city, the Marina District and North Beach.

3.1
First Reading

Read this selection quickly for the main ideas. Pay attention to the titles and the text headings as you read. Do *not* stop to look up words in your dictionary.

In a Collapsed Building, Heroism and the Promise of a Cup of Coffee

This article was written on the day of the San Francisco earthquake. It describes the rescue of a woman who was trapped in a building. Reprinted by permission of the *New York Times*, October 19, 1989.

1   SAN FRANCISCO, Oct. 18 — "Don't leave me — I don't want to die in here," a woman cried out to a San Francisco firefighter while trapped in a collapsed three-story apartment building about half an hour after the earthquake hit here Tuesday afternoon.

2   "I won't leave you," answered Jerry Shannon, the 44-year-old firefighter who had crawled into the rubble as the smoke of a fire that had broken out grew thicker and the sound of creaking wood beams overhead became more ominous. "And when this is over, we'll have a cup of coffee."

3   "I knew I didn't have much more time," Mr. Shannon would say later. "But I looked into her eyes, and I knew I couldn't leave her."

4 And for the next two and a half hours, he didn't, except for brief periods when he had to return to the street to get more equipment. At last he freed the woman, Sherra Cox, 55, from the beams that had pinned her. A stretcher was slid in, and she pushed with her feet and got onto it.

5 Outside, in the glow of fires, Ms. Cox, about to be put into an ambulance, reached up from her stretcher, grabbed Mr. Shannon's neck, pulled him to her and kissed him.

6 "You're my hero," she said.

7 "I owe you a cup of coffee," he replied.

8 "I owe you more than that," she said.

9 Then she was taken to the emergency ward of San Francisco General Hospital. Later, she would undergo surgery for a fractured pelvis. About that time, Mr. Shannon was tending to the cuts and bruises he had received during business hours in the night.

Not in City for Quake, Some Feel Left Out

This article was written four days after the San Francisco earthquake. It describes what happened to several North Beach families and how they felt about the disaster. Reprinted by permission of the *New York Times*, October 23, 1989.

1 SAN FRANCISCO Oct. 22 — For Margaret Boothroyd, returning home this weekend from the Adirondacks, New York, to her family's small apartment on Russian Hill was a little disorienting because everything looked the way it did before she left. Expecting to find half the city in ruin, she found herself instead looking out her bedroom window at her usual view of the brightly lighted Coit Tower to the east. As on any other night, neighbors were struggling up the steep hill with groceries and heading to the little Italian restaurants of nearby North Beach.

2 Ms. Boothroyd said her entire earthquake repair consisted of picking up stuffed animals belonging to her daughter Holly, which had fallen from a shelf. "Everything in the neighborhood is okay," she said.

3 Her experience is common here. After watching hours of television footage of the devastating fires and building collapses in the Marina district after Tuesday's earthquake, those finding

most of the city unchanged experienced a sense that the disaster happened on another planet.

A Feeling of Exclusion

4 "It's weird to come back because it feels completely normal," said Gordon Smith, Ms. Boothroyd's husband. Mr. Smith said the family had been visiting his father's cabin in Northville, New York, and learned of the quake when they turned on the television to watch the World Series [baseball game]. He said they called from 30 to 40 relatives, friends and coworkers in the last few days "and not one had anything happen to them or their houses."

5 For San Franciscans who carefully prepared for a quake of devastating magnitude but were out of town when it hit last week, there was also a feeling of exclusion from some sort of basic tribal experience, Mr. Smith said. He said that as he watched television from thousands of miles away, he felt "that's my town and I should be there; I want to be part of it." With announcements today that there are more volunteers than can be put to work at local shelters, Mr. Smith said the family does not know exactly what to do to help or to orient themselves to the death and loss that is reality in a small portion of the city. But they will not go walking in the Marina District. "We're not going to stare at other people's misery," he said.

6 Even in that neighborhood, long time residents are struggling to return their lives to rhythms that include joy and celebration.

7 When Stephanie Antonini walked down the aisle of St. Vincent De Paul Roman Catholic Church on Saturday afternoon to marry her childhood sweetheart, Geoffrey Mohun, she wore a long white satin dress and carried a bouquet of pink and white flowers, just as she had planned.

8 "We were determined we were going through with it," said Ms. Antonini, who grew up and lived in the Marina district until Tuesday night. After the quake forced her from her apartment, she moved in with her sister outside the district. She had to borrow clothing to wear to the rehearsal. Her wedding gown was the most important item she could retrieve in the brief moments she was permitted to return to her apartment before the wedding.

Visitors are Arriving

9 Some people are going forward with their plans to visit. Jeremy P.M. Thomas, on assignment here from England for a computer software company, persuaded his wife and two children not to cancel their plans to arrive today despite his own experience. After leaving his office when the tremors struck, Mr. Thomas experienced the three worst disasters of the earthquake in rapid succession on his commute home to North Beach.

10 After being turned back from his usual route to his apartment over the San Francisco-Oakland Bay Bridge [where a bridge section collapsed], he tried to drive south on the Nimitz Freeway only to be halted because of the collapse that trapped other commuters under tons of rubble. While listening to continuous tales of destruction on his car radio, he finally arrived home, only to find fires burning out of control in the Marina district.

11 "It was frightening," Mr Thomas said, "but the Californians have been so terribly nice. They keep apologizing, telling me, 'We're very sorry about this.'"

Reading Times	Reading Speed
1st reading _____ minutes	9 minutes = 111 wpm
3rd reading _____ minutes	8 minutes = 125 wpm
	7 minutes = 143 wpm
	6 minutes = 167 wpm
	5 minutes = 200 wpm

3.2
Second Reading

Go back and read the articles again. Take as much time as you need. Look up some of the unfamiliar words in the glossary at the end of this book or in your dictionary if you wish.

3.3
Third Reading

Read the articles quickly a third time. Concentrate on understanding the main ideas and the meanings of new vocabulary words in the context in which they appear.

3.4
Reader Response

In order to explore your response to this reading, write for 15 minutes about anything that interests you in this selection. You may wish to write about a personal experience this reading reminded you of — or you may wish to imagine how you might have handled the situations described in the reading. Try to explore *your own thoughts and feelings* as much as possible. Do *not* merely summarize or restate the ideas in the selection.

3.5
Response Sharing

Read your response to two or three other people in your class. Listen carefully to what the others have written. After you have discussed each other's responses, talk about other points of interest in the selection.

3.6
Identifying Main Ideas

Working with the same small group, make a list of the main ideas in this selection. Be sure to state the main ideas in your own words. Don't just copy sentences directly from the text. Think carefully about what the writer is trying to tell you.

3.7
Analyzing the Text

Work with your group members on this exercise. Discuss the answers carefully, particularly if there are disagreements among members of your group. In some cases, there may be more than one possible interpretation.

1. After Ms. Cox is rescued, Mr. Shannon says, "I owe you a cup of coffee." Ms. Cox answers, "I owe you more than that." What does "I owe you more than that" mean?

   a. "You saved my life."

   b. "I will pay you for saving me."

   c. "My house has been destroyed."

2. In "Not in City for Quake," in paragraph 1, Margaret Boothroyd felt strange because:

   a. her neighborhood was destroyed by the earthquake.

   b. the earthquake had not damaged her neighborhood at all.

   c. her neighbors were struggling up the steep hill.

3. According to paragraph 5, "there are more volunteers than can be put to work at local shelters" means:

   a. not enough people volunteered to help.

   b. so many people volunteered that the city didn't need all of them.

   c. volunteers didn't want to work at local shelters.

4. In paragraphs 7 and 8, the description of Stephanie Antonini shows that:

   a. she was very sad about the earthquake.

   b. she had to change all her wedding plans.

   c. she had lots of determination.

5. Read paragraphs 9, 10, and 11. Then write whether these statements are true (**T**) or false (**F**).

   a. _____ Mr. Thomas was a tourist in San Francisco.

   b. _____ Mr. Thomas drove over the San Francisco-Oakland Bay Bridge the night of the earthquake.

   c. _____ Mr. Thomas could not drive on the Nimitz Freeway.

   d. _____ The drive back to his home was frightening.

   e. _____ Mr. Thomas was angry at the way Californians acted after the earthquake.

6. In general, this reading describes:

    a. how much damage and unhappiness the earthquake caused.

    b. how angry people were that the earthquake had happened.

    c. how San Franciscans coped with the earthquake in their city.

    Why do you think so?

3.8
Vocabulary Study

Study the italicized words and phrases from "Not in City for Quake" in their contexts and guess their meanings. Write your guess on the first line. Then, look up the word or phrase in your dictionary and write the definition on the second line.

1. (paragraph 1) Expecting to find half the city in *ruin*, she found herself instead looking out her bedroom window at her usual view of the brightly lighted Coit Tower to the east.

    a. (guess) _____

    b. (dictionary) _____

2. (paragraph 1) As on any other night, neighbors were *struggling* up the steep hill with groceries....

    a. (guess) _____

    b. (dictionary) _____

3. (paragraph 5) For San Franciscans who...were out of town when it hit last week, there was also a feeling of *exclusion* from some sort of basic tribal experience, Mr. Smith said.

    a. (guess) _____

    b. (dictionary) _____

4. (paragraph 6) Even in that neighborhood, long time residents are struggling to return their lives to rhythms that include joy and *celebration*.

    a. (guess) _____

    b. (dictionary) _____

5. (paragraph 8) We were *determined* we were going through with it.... She had to borrow clothing to wear to the rehearsal. Her wedding gown was the most important item she could retrieve in the brief moments she was permitted to return to her apartment before the wedding.

    a. (guess) _____

    b. (dictionary) _____

3.9
What Does "It" Refer To?

In several sentences in these readings, the word "it" is used to refer back to some other word, situation, or event. Read these sentences, then look back in the texts to find out what "it" is referring to. Discuss your answers with your small group.

1. (paragraph 4 of "Ms. Cox") At last he freed the woman, Sherra Cox, 55, from the beams that had pinned her. A stretcher was slid in, and she pushed with her feet and got onto *it*.

    a. the beams   b. her feet   c. a stretcher

2. (paragraph 1 of "Not in City for Quake") For Margaret Boothroyd, returning home this weekend from the Adirondacks, New York, to her family's small apartment on Russian Hill was a little disorienting because everything looked the way *it* did before she left.

    a. everything in her apartment

    b. the Adirondacks

    c. brightly lit Coit Tower

3. (paragraph 5) For San Franciscans who carefully prepared for a quake of devastating magnitude but were out of town when *it* hit last week, there was also a feeling of exclusion from some sort of basic tribal experience.

    a. tribal experience   b. the earthquake   c. San Francisco

4. (paragraph 5) He said that as he watched television from thousands of miles away, he felt "that's my town and I should be there; I want to be part of *it*."

    a. the earthquake experience

    b. watching television

    c. a small portion of the city

5. (paragraph 8) "We were determined we were going through with *it*," said Ms. Antonini, who grew up and lived in the Marina District until Tuesday night.

   a. Marina District

   b. a long white satin dress

   c. her wedding

6. (paragraph 11) "*It* was frightening," Mr. Thomas said, "but the Californians have been so terribly nice."

   a. the earthquake

   b. his family's visit

   c. computer software company

3.10
Application, Critical Evaluation, and Synthesis

In these readings, the people express their feelings about the earthquake experience. Think about each of the following quotes and write your reaction to it. What do you think the person means? Would you feel that way if you were a resident of San Francisco? Why? (See page 171 and page 172 in the Expansion section on how to use quotes and paraphrasing.)

1. "I knew I didn't have much more time. But I looked into her eyes, and I knew I couldn't leave her." (paragraph 3 of "Ms. Cox")

2. "It's weird to come back because it feels completely normal." (paragraph 4 of "Not in City for Quake")

3. "That's my town and I should be there; I want to be part of it." (paragraph 5)

4. "We're not going to stare at other people's misery." (paragraph 5)

5. "We were determined we were going through with [our wedding]." (paragraph 8)

6. "The Californians have been so terribly nice. They keep apologizing, telling me, 'We're very sorry about this.' " (paragraph 11)

AT THE END OF EVERY UNIT, YOU ARE INVITED TO TURN TO THE EXPANSION SECTION ON PAGE 155. THIS SECTION CONCENTRATES ON SOME OF THE FUNDAMENTALS OF WRITING.

Across Many Cultures

Every society has social customs that people use to interact with each other. Customs vary in different societies. In fact, what is polite or correct in one society may be unacceptable in another. When we live in or visit other societies, it is important to understand the local customs. Misunderstandings often arise if we we expect customs to be the same everywhere.

Discussion

Before you begin reading, think about the following questions and discuss your answers.

1. In your country, where can people get advice when they have problems? List the ways they get advice. Then compare your list with several classmates. Do any of the items on their lists surprise you? If so, explain why they surprise you. Are you surprised that some things are *not* on their lists? Ask them several questions about why they do not get advice in these ways.

2. Are advice columns in newspapers or magazines popular in your country? If so, what kinds of topics do people write about?

3. In your country, if you receive a dinner invitation to a friend's house for 7:00 P.M., what time would you arrive? Would you bring a gift? If yes, what would you bring? If no, why not? How late would you stay? What would you do when you leave? Would you feel an obligation to invite your friend to your house for dinner? How would you answer these questions if the invitation was to the home of your boss? Make a class chart using the outline on the next page.

THE DINNER INVITATION SAYS 7:00 P.M.

Country	I Arrive	Gift?	Leave at (time)? What Do You Do?	Obligation to Invite?
USA				
friend:	7-7:15 P.M.	not necessary, but might bring wine, candy, or cake	10-10:30 P.M. Shake hands, maybe kiss	No, but I probably want to.
boss:	7-7:15 P.M.	No	9:30-10 P.M. Shake hands	No

4. In your country, how do men and women typically choose the person they will marry? What happens if a person doesn't follow the typical custom?

Puzzled writer takes a swipe at clearing guilty conscience

DEAR ABBY: In a recent column, a woman wrote to say that one of her guests at a dinner party had stolen a fork, and she didn't know how to go about recovering it.

I wasn't that guest, but over the last 10 years I have taken three items from homes where I have been a guest. Abby, I cannot for the life of me understand why I took these things! I have pondered and pondered as to how I can get these items back to the homes from which I took them.

I can't come out openly and admit that I took them. This is a small town, and I am well known here. If just one of these people talked about it, I would be finished!

Abby, what's wrong with me? They are really insignificant items. I thought about seeing some kind of counselor, but in a town like this, should I be seen going into the office of a therapist or any professional counselor, it would be all over town in no time. Secretaries talk, nurses talk and psychotherapists talk, too. You would be amazed at how unprofessional their conduct is in a small town.

I'll bet there are thousands of people like me who wish they had the nerve to return something. Should I just wait until it's dark, then put the items in the mailboxes of their rightful owners?
— Guilty conscience

DEAR GUILTY CONSCIENCE:

DEAR ABBY

ABIGAIL VAN BUREN
Syndicated columnist

Yes. It will relieve your conscience, but it will not solve your problem. You need to seek professional help to find out why you took those items so you won't continue that behavior. See a therapist in another town or city nearby to protect your privacy.

You are probably a kleptomaniac — a person who has a neurotic compulsion to steal without economic motive.

Please take my advice, and let me hear from you again. I care.

DEAR ABBY: Recently I attended a luncheon buffet with co-workers when the issue of tipping arose.

One co-worker did not leave a tip, while another co-worker left a generous tip.

The server took drink orders, made sure the water glasses were always filled and removed the dishes; payment was made at the table.

An ongoing argument ensued. In such a situation, what is the appropriate tipping etiquette? We have agreed to abide by your advice.
— Jill Ann Maynor, West Chester, Ohio

DEAR JILL: There should be no question about the tipping at a buffet. The server should be tipped 10 percent by each diner. The guest who left nothing should be ashamed.

DEAR ABBY: When my granddaughter kept ordering her dogs to "lay down," I told her she should say "LIE down."

"No wonder they don't mind me!" she said.
— Gertrude Miler, Olympia, Wash.

CONFIDENTIAL TO HELEN THOMAS: Happy birthday, friend!

C H A P T E R   O N E

Tell Me Your Problem

When some people have personal problems, they write to the advice columns in the newspaper. These columns can give us insights into how people in different cultures handle their problems. Read this article and think if you would give the same answers as the advice columnists. "Dear Abby" letters taken from a DEAR ABBY column by Abigail Van Buren. © 1990 Universal Press Syndicate. Reprinted with permission. All rights reserved.

1.1
First Reading

Read this article quickly for the main ideas. Pay attention to the title and the advice given to each person. Do *not* stop to look up words in your dictionary.

1   What do you do if you have a personal problem? Do you talk to your mother or father, a sister or brother, a friend, a minister? What if you are embarrassed to talk to them — or you think they won't be sympathetic? Newspapers all over the world have advice columns to help readers solve their problems. Do you agree with the following advice?

2   In Japan, most of the letter writers are women, and their most common complaint is about living with their mothers-in-law. The writers rarely get a lot of sympathy. They are often told to put up with the problem and to find some good point in it. For example, one housewife complained that her husband will not let her handle the household money. He gives his whole paycheck to his mother who lives with them. She says she feels like "a nobody" in her own house. The columnist gave this advice: "This has always been a common problem between wives and mothers-in-law, and you have a good reason to be miserable. But you should consider yourself lucky that you don't have to worry about the family budget. You have time to do other things and enjoy yourself."

3   Sometimes the letter writers in Japan are told to change their own behavior. A young woman complained that her older brother was lazy. She was told "it is your own fault because you treat him like a child."

4   While very few newspapers in China have advice columns, they do exist. The letters are mostly from women, who have very few places to turn for advice. They often write about unhappy marriages, interfering mothers-in-law, and parent-child relationships. Other readers write about money matters and medical problems; some elderly parents complain that their children will not support them.

5   In advice to those with marital problems, one columnist says she tries to preserve marriages because they are important for China's development. To one man who left his wife and children for another married woman, she advised: "You did not treasure your happy and legal family relationships and have betrayed your wife and recklessly broken up two families.... I hope other readers will draw lessons from your mistakes."

6   In the United States, a popular advice column is "Dear Abby." Many of the letters to "Dear Abby" also deal with marriage and in-laws. Here are some letters to "Dear Abby."

7   DEAR ABBY:

My son is engaged to a girl I'll call Lucy. Lucy has eaten dinner at our house every Sunday for the last seven months. I fix good meals and she eats heartily and acts like she enjoys the meal, but she has never once offered to help me with the dishes, or even take her plate into the kitchen. My son says Lucy is a guest and she's not supposed to. I say he's wrong. What do you say?—(Signed) A difference of opinion.

DEAR DIFFERENCE:

Who's right and who's wrong is not nearly as important as developing a good relationship with your future daughter-in-law. Try treating Lucy more like a member of the family than a guest. For openers, after dinner, say, "Let's clear the table — many hands make light work." Or, "How about giving me a hand with these dishes, Lucy? It's been a long day; besides I'd appreciate the company." It will make Lucy feel useful and will do wonders for your relationship with your future daughter-in-law.

8   DEAR ABBY:

Our son, age 32, is marrying a woman who is 23. It's his second marriage and her first, and I know she's planning a big church wedding. We are reluctant to send invitations to our friends and relatives who attended our son's first wedding and sent lovely gifts. Would it be proper to enclose a little note with the invitations to those who have already given him one wedding gift saying that no gift is expected? — (Signed) Pondering parents.

DEAR PARENTS:

Please resist enclosing a little note with the wedding invitations. Consider the bride. It's her first wedding and she shouldn't be deprived of gifts because it's her husband's second.

Reading Times	**Reading Speed**
1st reading _____ minutes	5 minutes = 136 wpm
3rd reading _____ minutes	4 minutes = 170 wpm
	3 minutes = 227 wpm
	2 minutes = 340 wpm

1.2
Second Reading

Go back and read the selection again. Take as much time as you need. Look up some of the unfamiliar words in the glossary at the end of this book or in your dictionary if you wish.

1.3
Third Reading

Read the selection quickly a third time. Concentrate on understanding the main ideas and the meanings of new vocabulary words in the context in which they appear.

1.4
Reader Response

In order to explore your response to this reading, write for 15 minutes about anything that interests you in this selection. You may wish to write about a personal experience or advice column this reading reminded you of — or you may wish to agree or disagree with something in the reading. Try to explore *your own thoughts and feelings* as much as possible. Do *not* merely summarize or restate the ideas in the selection.

1.5
Response Sharing

Read your response to two or three other people in your class. Listen carefully to what the others have written. After you have discussed each other's responses, talk about other points of interest in the selection.

1.6
Identifying Main Ideas

Working with the same small group, make a list of the main ideas in this selection. Be sure to state the main ideas in your own words. Don't just copy sentences directly from the text. Think carefully about what the writer is trying to tell you.

1.7
Analyzing the Text

Work with your group members on this exercise. Discuss the answers carefully, particularly if there are disagreements among members of your group. In some cases, there may be more than one possible interpretation.

1. In paragraph 2, why does the wife feel like a "nobody" in her own house?

   a. She has no responsibility.

   b. Her mother-in-law doesn't like her.

   c. She has a lot of free time.

   Why do you think so?

2. In paragraph 2, the advice given to the wife is an example of:

   a. the second sentence in the paragraph ("The writers rarely get a lot of sympathy.")

   b. the third sentence ("They are often told to put up with the problem and to find some good point in it.")

   c. both a and b.

   Why do you think so?

3. In paragraph 5, the columnist is _____ to the man who wrote to her.

   a. not sympathetic
   b. sympathetic
   c. neutral

4. In paragraph 7, Dear Abby says "Who's right and who's wrong is not nearly as important as developing a good relationship with your future daughter-in-law." Abby is suggesting that the family:

   a. blame the daughter-in-law.
   b. find a solution that keeps everyone happy.
   c. stop inviting Lucy over for dinner.

5. In Dear Abby's answer in paragraph 8, Abby:

   a. is opposed to second marriages.
   b. agrees with the parents.
   c. is sympathetic to the bride.

1.8
Vocabulary Study

Study the italicized words and phrases in their contexts and guess their meanings. Write your guess on the first line. Then, look up the word or phrase in your dictionary and write the definition on the second line.

1. (paragraph 2) The writers rarely get a lot of sympathy. They are often told to *put up with* the problem and to find some good point in it.

   a. (guess) _____

   b. (dictionary) _____

2. (paragraph 5) "You did not *treasure* your happy and legal family relationships and have betrayed your wife and recklessly broken up two families...."

   a. (guess) _____

   b. (dictionary) _____

3. (paragraph 7) I fix good meals and she eats *heartily* and acts like she enjoys the meal.

    a. (guess) _____

    b. (dictionary) _____

4. (paragraph 7) "How about *giving me a hand* with these dishes, Lucy? It's been a long day; besides I'd appreciate the company."

    a. (guess) _____

    b. (dictionary) _____

5. (paragraph 8) Please resist enclosing a little note with the wedding invitations. Consider the bride. It's her first wedding and she shouldn't *be deprived of* gifts because it's her husband's second.

    a. (guess) _____

    b. (dictionary) _____

1.9
Dictionary Study: Words in Context

Words may have more than one meaning. Look up each italicized word in the dictionary entries given here. Decide which meaning is used in the sentence. Then write the meaning on the line below the sentence. Discuss your answers with your small group.

1. Newspapers all over the world have advice *columns* to help readers solve their problems.

    _____

2. In Japan, most of the letter writers are women, and their most *common* complaint is about living with their mothers-in-law.

    _____

3. They are often told to put up with the problem and to find some good *point* in it.

    _____

4. For example, one housewife complained that her husband will not let her *handle* the household money.

_____

5. She was told "it is your own fault because you *treat* him like a child."

_____

6. I hope other readers will *draw* lessons from your mistakes.

_____

7. I *fix* good meals and she eats heartily and acts like she enjoys the meal....

_____

8. For openers, after dinner, say, "Let's clear the table — many hands make *light* work."

---

col-umn (kŏl'əm) *n.* **1.** A supporting pillar consisting of a base, a cylindrical shaft, and a capital. **2.** Something resembling a column in form or function: *a column of mercury in a thermometer.* **3. a.** One of two or more vertical sections of typed lines lying side by side on a page and separated by a rule or blank space. **b.** A feature article that appears regularly in a newspaper or other periodical. **4.** A formation, as of troops or vehicles, in which all elements follow one behind the other. **5.** *Bot.* An organ formed by the fusion of stamens or of stamens and pistils, as in the orchid. [ME *columne* < Lat. *columna*] **—col'umned** (kŏl'əmd) *adj.*

com-mon (kŏm'ən) *adj.* **-er, -est. 1. a.** Belonging equally to or shared equally by two or more; joint: *common interests.* **b.** Of or pertaining to the community as a whole; public: *the common good.* **2.** Widespread; prevalent; general: *common knowledge.* **3. a.** Of frequent or habitual occurrence; usual: *a common phenomenon.* **b.** Most widely known or occurring most frequently; ordinary: *the common crow.* **4.** Without special designation, status, or rank: *a common sailor.* **5. a.** Not distinguished by superior or other characteristics; average: *the common spectator.* **b.** Of no special quality; standard: *common procedure.* **c.** Of mediocre or inferior quality; second-rate: *common cloth.* **6.** Unrefined or coarse in manner; vulgar: *behavior that branded him as common.* **7.** *Gram.* **a.** Either masculine or feminine in gender. **b.** Representing one or all the members of a class; not designating a unique entity. — *n.* **1. commons.** The common people; commonalty. **2. commons.** *(used with a sing. or pl. verb)*, **a.** The political class comprising the commoners. **b.** The parliamentary representatives of this class. **c.** Often **Commons.** The House of Commons. **3.** A tract of land belonging to or used by a community as a whole. **4.** The legal right of a person to use the lands or waters of another, as for fishing. **5. commons.** *(used with a sing. verb).* A building or hall for dining. **6.** *Eccles.* A service used for a particular class of festivals. **—idiom. in common.** Equally with or by all. —See Usage note at **mutual.** [ME *commune* < O Fr. < Lat. *communis.*] — **com'mon-ly** *adv.* **—com'mon-ness** *n.*

draw (drô) *v.* **drew** (dro͞o), **drawn** (drôn), **draw-ing, draws.** *—tr.* **1. a.** To cause to move after or toward one by applying continuous force; pull; drag. **b.** To cause to move in a given direction or to a given position, as by leading: *She drew us into the room.* **c.** To move or pull so as to cover or uncover: *draw the drapes.* **2.** To cause to flow forth: *a pump drawing water.* **3.** To suck or take in (air); inhale. **4.** To displace (a specified depth of water) in floating: *a boat drawing 18 inches.* **5. a.** To take or pull out: *drew the gun from his belt.* **b.** to eviscerate; disembowel. **c.** To extract or take from for one's own use: *drew strength from her example.* **6. a.** To allure or attract: *afraid the casino will draw undesirable elements to the town.* **b.** To select or take in from a given group, type, or region: *draw clients from all levels of society.* **7. a.** To induce to act: *Frustration drew me into the squabble.* **b.** To bring on oneself as a result; provoke: *drew enemy fire.* **c.** To evoke as a response, elicit; *drew jeers and taunts from the audience.* **8. a.** To earn or bring in: *draw interest.* **b.** To withdraw (money). **c.** To use (a check, for example) when paying. **d.** To receive on a regular basis or at a specified time: *draw a salary.* **9.** To take or receive by chance: *draw lots.* **10. a.** To take (cards) from a dealer or central stack. **b.** To force (a card) to be played. **11.** To end or leave (a contest) tied or undecided. **12.** To hit or strike (a ball) so as to give it backspin. **13.** To pull back the string of (a bow). **14.** To distort the shape of. **15.** To stretch taut. **16. a.** To flatten, stretch, or mold (metal) by hammering or die stamping. **b.** To shape or elongate (a wire, for example) by drawing through dies. **17. a.** To describe (a line or figure) with a drafting implement. **b.** To draft or sketch (a picture). **18. a.** To portray by writing, speech, or imitative actions: *a poet who draws moving scenes of ghetto life.* **b.** To formulate or devise from the evidence or data at hand: *draw a comparison.*

fix (fĭks) *v.* **fixed, fix·ing, fix·es.** —*tr.* **1. a.** To place or fasten securely. **b.** To make fast to; attach. **2.** To put into a stable or unalterable form, as: **a.** *Chem.* To make (a substance) nonvolatile or solid. **b.** *Biol.* To convert (nitrogen) into stable, biologically assimilable compounds. **c.** To kill and keep (a specimen) intact for microscopic study. **d.** To prevent discoloration of (a photographic image) by washing or coating with a chemical preservative. **3.** To direct steadily: *fixed her eyes on the page.* **4.** To establish definitely: *fix a time.* **5.** To assign: *fixing the blame.* **6.** To set right; adjust. **7.** *Computer Sci.* To convert data from floating-point notation to fixed-point notation. **8.** To restore to proper condition or working order; repair. **9.** To make ready; prepare. **10.** To spay or castrate (an animal). **11.** *Informal.* To take revenge upon; get even with. **12.** To influence or arrange the outcome of by unlawful means. —*intr.* **1.** To become concentrated, directed, or attached. **2.** To become stable or firm; harden. **3.** *Regional.* To intend: *was fixing to take the children with her.* —*n.* **1.** A difficult or embarrassing position; predicament. **2.** The position, as of a ship or aircraft, as determined by observations or radio. **3.** An instance of arranging for special consideration or exemption from a requirement, esp. by means of bribery. **4.** *Slang.* An intravenous injection of a narcotic. [ME *fixen* < *fix,* fixed in position < Lat. *fixus,* p.part of *figere,* to fasten.] —**fix'a·ble** *adj.* —**fix'er** *n.*

han·dle (hăn'dl) *v.* **-dled, -dling, -dles.** —*tr.* **1.** To touch, lift, or hold with the hands. **2.** To operate with the hands; manipulate. **3.** To deal with or have the responsibility for; conduct: *handle corporation law.* **4. a.** To direct, execute, or dispose of: *handle an investment.* **b.** To manage, administer to, or represent: *handle a boxer.* **5.** To confront or cope with: *handle a crowd; handle a problem.* **6.** To deal or trade in the purchase or sale of: *the branch office that handles grain exports.* —*intr.* To act or function under operation: *a car that handles well in the snow.* —*n.* **1.** A part that is designed to be held or operated with the hand. **2.** An opportunity or means for achieving a purpose. **3.** *Slang.* A person's name. **4.** The total amount of money bet on an event or over a set period of time. [ME *handelen* < OE *handlian.*]

light² (lĭt) *adj.* **-er, est. 1. a.** Of relatively little weight; not heavy. **b.** Of relatively little weight for its size or bulk: *Titanium is a light metal.* **c.** Of less than the correct, standard, or legal weight: *a light pound.* **2.** Exerting little force or impact; gentle: *a light pat.* **3. a.** Of little quantity; scanty: *light snow.* **b.** Consuming or using relatively moderate amounts; abstemious: *a light eater; a light smoker.* **4.** Requiring little effort or exertion: *light household tasks.* **5.** Having little importance; insignificant: *light chatter.* **6.** Intended primarily as entertainment; not serious or profound: *a light comedy.* **7.** Free from worries or troubles; blithe: *a light heart.* **8.** Characterized by frivolity. **9.** Liable to change; fickle. **10.** Mildly dizzy: *felt light in the head.* **11.** Lacking in

sexual discrimination; wanton. **12.** Moving easily and quickly; nimble: *light and graceful on her feet.* **13.** Designed for ease and quickness of movement: *a light airplane.* **14.** Carrying little weight. **15.** Carrying little equipment or arms: *light cavalry.* **16.** Requiring relatively little equipment and utilizing relatively simple processes: *light industry.* **17.** Easily awakened or disturbed: *a light sleeper.* **18. a.** Easily digested: *a light supper.* **b.** Having a spongy or flaky texture; well-leavened: *light pastries.* **19.** Having a loose, porous consistency: *light earth.* **20.** Containing a relatively small amount of alcohol: *a light wine.* **21.** Designating a vowel or syllable pronounced with little or no stress. —*adv.* **-er, -est. 1.** Lightly. **2.** With little weight and few burdens: *traveling light.* —*intr.v.* **light·ed** or **lit** (lĭt), **light·ing, lights. 1.** To get down, as from a horse; dismount. **2.** To come to rest; alight. **3.** To come upon one unexpectedly: *Misfortune lighted upon him.* **4.** To come upon by chance or accident. —*phrasal verbs.* **light into.** To attack verbally or physically; assail. **light out.** To leave hastily; run off. —*idiom.* **make light of.** To regard or treat as insignificant or petty. [ME < OE *lēoht.*]

point (point) *n.* **1.** The sharp or tapered end of something. **2.** Something that has a sharp or tapered end, as a knife or needle. **3.** A tapering extension of land projecting into water; cape. **4.** A mark formed by or as if by the sharp end of something. **5.** A mark or dot used in printing or writing. **6.** A mark used in punctuation, esp. a period. **7.** A decimal point. **8.** The vowel point. **9.** One of the protruding marks used in certain methods of writing and printing for the blind. **10.** *Math.* A dimensionless geometric object having no property but location. **11.** A position, place, or locality; spot: *a good point to begin; connections to Chicago and points west.* **12.** A specified degree, condition, or limit, as in a scale or course. **13. a.** Any of the 32 equal divisions marked at the circumference of a mariner's compass card that indicate direction. **b.** The distance or interval of 11 degrees, 15 minutes between any two adjacent markings. **14.** A distinct condition or degree: *the point of no return.* **15.** A specific moment in time: *At this point, we are ready to proceed.* **16.** A crucial situation in a course of events. **17.** An important, essential, or primary factor. **18.** A purpose, goal, advantage, or reason: *What's the point of discussing it?* **19.** The major idea or essential part of a concept or narrative. **20.** A significant, outstanding, or effective idea, argument, or suggestion. **21.** A separate or individual item or element; detail.

treat (trēt) *v.* **treat·ed, treat·ing, treats.** —*tr.* **1.** To act or behave in a specified manner toward. **2.** To regard or consider in a certain way: *treated her as a sister.* **3.** To deal with in writing or speech; expound: *an article that treats all aspects of nuclear power.* **4.** To deal with or represent in a specified manner or style, as in art or literature: *treat a subject poetically.* **5.** To entertain at one's own expense: *treat her to the theater.* **6.** To subject to a process, action or change, esp.: **a.** To give medical aid to. **b.** To subject to a chemical or physical process or application. —*intr.* **1.** To deal with a subject or topic in writing, speaking, or thought: *The essay treats of courtly love.* **2.** To pay for another's entertainment, food, or the like. **3.** To negotiate; bargain. —*n.* **1.** Something, as food or entertainment, generously paid for by someone else. **2.** The act of providing a treat, esp. in return. **3.** Something considered a special delight or pleasure. [ME *treten* < AN *treter* < Lat. *tractare,* freq. of *trahere,* to draw.] —**treat'a·ble** *adj.* —**treat'er** *n.*

1.10
Application, Critical Evaluation, and Synthesis

1. When people have personal problems in your country, how do they typically solve them? Whom do they talk to? Are they comfortable talking to family, friends, or professional counselors? Are they expected to put up with the problem and not complain? Give some examples of your answers.

2. Are advice columns popular in your country? Who reads them? Who writes letters to them? What kinds of questions do people ask? What kinds of answers do the columnists give? If you can, give some examples.

3. a. Choose one of the situations in this selection. If you were an advice columnist, what advice would you give to the person? Why would you give that advice?

    b. Now interview one of your classmates. What advice would she or he give the person? Develop some questions to ask this "advice columnist" (see page 175) and conduct the interview (page 175). Then use the interview information to write a short report (page 176). Be sure to use some quotes and paraphrasing (pages 171–172). Share this report with your class.

"Dear Abby..."

"When in Rome, do as the Romans do."

What is polite in one country may be impolite in another country. This reading describes some customs from four different countries. The reading is excerpted from the *N.Y. Times* Travel Section of March 11, 1984. The saying "When in Rome, do as the Romans do" means that you should follow local customs, even if they are different from the customs in your home country. Reprinted by permission of the *New York Times*.

2.1
First Reading

Read this selection quickly for the main ideas. Pay attention to the title and the variety of customs as you read. Do *not* stop to look up words in your dictionary.

1   In Latin American countries, it is customary to be late for appointments. The Swedes expect people to arrive precisely on time. In Egypt, even the smallest service should be rewarded with a tip. Japan is virtually a no-tipping society. In Mexico, courtesy requires that you inquire about one's spouse and family. In Saudi Arabia, such a question would be an intrusion of privacy.

2   How can travelers "do as the Romans do"? A survey of well-traveled people from other countries who now live in the United States produced this advice.

3   **Japan.** While bowing is the customary greeting, the handshake is acceptable these days, says Etsuko Penner of the Japanese National Tourist Organization, but the foreigner is advised to wait and see what the Japanese does. If he or she extends a hand, shake it, but if greeted by a bow, it's better to return one, bending from the waist, with the hands at your sides. Sightseers should remember to remove their shoes on entering any religious place or a private home. Invitations to

Japanese homes are rare, since the Japanese see them as private, modest and unsuitable for entertaining guests; they prefer to entertain outside the home. Eating on the street is frowned upon, although increasing numbers of young people do it, partly because of the growth of American-style fast food places. At the table, lay chopsticks on the table; never leave them in a bowl. Travelers do not tip taxi drivers. Hairdressers do not get tips, and neither does a chambermaid, unless she is asked to perform a specific errand. What you do then, says Mrs. Penner of the tourist organization, is to wrap [the money] in a piece of paper and give it to her. To pass money "nakedly" would be demeaning. As for gifts, they are not opened when they are given. So do not be disappointed by the absence of oohs and ahs.

4   **Sweden.** An invitation for 7 P.M. means you must arrive precisely at 7. "It's not uncommon for guests to make sure they get to the right place on time by arriving 15 minutes early and then walk around the block or, in an apartment building, wait downstairs until the exact hour," says Swedish-born Mona Staaf. "You shake hands when you say hello and when you say good-bye, and it's considered good manners to shake hands on leaving before, not after, you put on your coat." Miss Staaf, who is the front office manager of the Interlaken Inn in Lakeville, Conn., adds, "There's very little kissing, except between very close relatives, and it's not unusual for sisters to greet each other with a handshake." Dinner guests in private homes should arrive with flowers — with the wrapping removed — or a box of chocolates, not wine (which is relatively expensive in Sweden). The honored guest will be placed at the hostess's left. Before leaving the table, thank the hosts for the meal and telephone the next day to say thank you again.

5   **Mexico**. "A smile and handshake will go a long way in Mexico," says Vincent Hodgins of the Mexican National Tourist Council, "but a gentleman should never ever attempt to kiss a woman he doesn't know well, either on the face or on the hand." While it seems that everyone is embracing, kissing is only for those with long-standing friendships. In the country of mãnana, your host will expect you to be 15 to 30 minutes late for lunch or dinner; women invited on their own are never expected to arrive on time. Chivalry is very much alive, and men open doors of cars and buildings for women. They are expected to stand when a woman enters a room and to give up their seat on buses and on the subway. It is generally considered in poor taste to wear shorts on city streets and for women to wear slacks to any social gathering. If you should be invited to spend the weekend at a Mexican's home, sending flowers to the hostess is considered preferable to arriving with a gift.

6   **Egypt.** If you admire a possession or an article of clothing, says Nimet Habachy, the host of the WQXR "New York at Night" program, it is likely to be offered to you. It is a custom, "part formula and part generosity," that confounds many visitors. They should use discretion about whether to accept the offering. Miss Habachy, a native of Cairo, recommends that women dress conservatively in public places. "For Westerners, especially women, to walk around without sleeves is not a good move, and shorts are out. Many mosques, especially those off

the usual tour beat, do not welcome women; and visitors, on entering a mosque, should remove their shoes and put on the over-sock that is provided. "Remember, too, that tips are the only source of income for many people. A tip is expected for the least service. That is the way it is."

Reading Times	**Reading Speed**
1st reading _____ minutes	7 minutes = 120 wpm
3rd reading _____ minutes	6 minutes = 140 wpm
	5 minutes = 168 wpm
	4 minutes = 210 wpm
	3 minutes = 280 wpm

2.2
Second Reading

Go back and read the selection again. Take as much time as you need. Look up some of the unfamiliar words in the glossary at the end of this book or in your dictionary if you wish.

2.3
Third Reading

Read the selection quickly a third time. Concentrate on understanding the main ideas and the meanings of new vocabulary words in the context in which they appear.

2.4
Reader Response

In order to explore your response to this reading, write for 15 minutes about anything that interests you in this selection. You may wish to write about a personal experience this reading reminded you of — or you may wish to agree or disagree with something in the reading. Try to explore *your own thoughts and feelings* as much as possible. Do *not* merely summarize or restate the ideas in the selection.

2.5
Response Sharing

Read your response to two or three other people in your class. Listen carefully to what the others have written. After you have discussed each other's responses, talk about other points of interest in the selection.

2.6
Identifying Main Ideas

Working with the same small group, make a list of the main ideas in this selection. Be sure to state the main ideas in your own words. Don't just copy sentences directly from the text. Think carefully about what the writer is trying to tell you.

2.7
Analyzing the Text

Work with your group members on this exercise. Discuss the answers carefully, particularly if there are disagreements among members of your group. In some cases, there may be more than one possible interpretation.

1. Paragraph 1 gives examples of different customs:
    a. to show how unusual they are.
    b. to introduce what the article will be about.
    c. to get you interested in the topic.
    d. a and b.
    e. b and c.
    f. a, b, and c.

2. (paragraph 3) "The foreigner is advised to wait and see what the Japanese does. If **he or she** extends a hand, shake **it**, but if greeted by a bow, it's better to return **one**, bending from the waist, with **the** hands at your sides." What does each boldfaced word refer to?
    a. **he or she**: a foreigner — a Japanese person — Etsuko Penner
    b. **it**: hand — waist — person
    c. **one**: person — handshake — bow
    d. **the**: your — the other person's

3. According to paragraph 6, in Egypt, if you admire something that belongs to a person, it might be offered to you. Should you accept it?

   a. Yes, definitely accept it.

   b. No, never accept it.

   c. Think carefully and decide for yourself.

   How do you know?

4. The writer of this article:

   a. is neutral to the customs of all the countries and doesn't make any judgments.

   b. thinks some countries' customs are better than the customs of other countries.

   c. is critical of all the customs because they are different from American customs.

   Why do you think so?

5. In the countries described in this article, some customs are similar and others are different. Explain what each statement below says about that country. Then compare the two statements; are they similar or different?

   Tipping:
   a. To pass money "nakedly" would be demeaning. (paragraph 3)

   b. A tip is expected for the least service. That's the way it is. (paragraph 6)

   Kissing:
   a. There's very little kissing except between very close relatives. (paragraph 4)

   b. A gentleman should never attempt to kiss a woman he doesn't know well. (paragraph 5)

   Find at least two more contrasts in the customs of these countries. Write the sentences and explain how they differ.

2.8
Vocabulary Study

Study the italicized words and phrases in their contexts and guess their meanings. Write your guess on the first line. Then, look up the word or phrase in your dictionary and write the definition on the second line.

1. (paragraph 3) If he or she *extends* a hand, shake it, but if greeted by a bow, it's better to return one....

    a. (guess) _____

    b. (dictionary) _____

2. (paragraph 3) Invitations to Japanese homes are *rare*, since the Japanese see them as private, modest and unsuitable for entertaining guests; they prefer to entertain outside the home.

    a. (guess) _____

    b. (dictionary) _____

3. (paragraph 4) An invitation for 7 P.M. means you must arrive *precisely* at 7. It's not uncommon for guests to make sure they get to the right place on time by arriving 15 minutes early and then walk around the block or, in an apartment building, wait downstairs until the exact hour.

    a. (guess) _____

    b. (dictionary) _____

4. (paragraph 4) Dinner guests in private homes should arrive with flowers—with the wrapping removed—or a box of chocolates, not wine (which is *relatively* expensive in Sweden).

    a. (guess) _____

    b. (dictionary) _____

5. (paragraph 6) Miss Habachy, a native of Cairo, recommends that women dress *conservatively* in public places. "For Westerners, especially women, to walk around without sleeves is not a good move, and shorts are out."

    a. (guess) _____

    b. (dictionary) _____

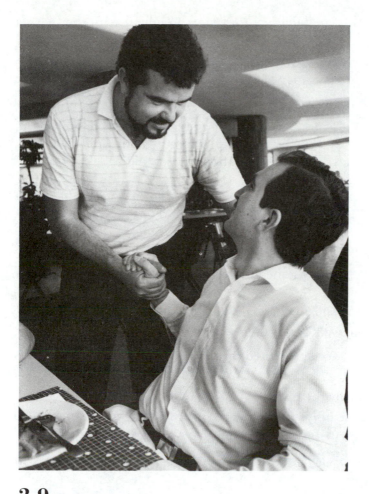

2.9
Special Expressions

The words and phrases in italics have special meanings. Study them in context in their paragraphs. Then, working with your small group, choose the best answer for each one. Check your answers in your glossary or dictionary.

1. (paragraph 3) Don't be disappointed by the absence of *oohs and ahs*.

   a. The Japanese will not make complimentary remarks about the gift when you give it to them.

   b. The Japanese will apologize that they don't have a gift for you.

   c. The Japanese will not tell you if they don't like the gift.

   What are "oohs and ahs"?

2. (paragraph 4) It's *not unusual* for sisters to greet each other with a handshake.

   a. Sisters often greet each other with a handshake.
   b. Sisters rarely greet each other with a handshake.
   c. Sisters do not greet each other with a handshake.

3. (paragraph 4) It is *not uncommon* for guests to make sure they get to the right place on time by arriving 15 minutes early and then walk around the block...until the exact hour.

   a. It is very rare.
   b. It is never done.
   c. It happens often.

4. (paragraph 5) A smile and a handshake *will go a long way* in Mexico.

   a. You have to know someone well before you can shake his or her hand.
   b. Smiling and shaking hands is the best thing to do.
   c. You should walk across the room to shake hands.

5. (paragraph 5) Women invited *on their own* are never expected to arrive on time.

   a. They come by themselves.
   b. They are the only guest.
   c. They are invited for the first time.

6. (paragraph 5) It is generally considered *in poor taste* to wear shorts on city streets....

   a. Wearing shorts shows good judgment.
   b. Only people without money wear shorts.
   c. It is bad manners to wear shorts.

7. (paragraph 6) For Westerners, especially women, to walk around without sleeves *is not a good move*, and shorts are *out*.

   not a good move:
   a. It is not comfortable to wear clothes without sleeves.
   b. Westerners without sleeves should go away.
   c. It's not a sensible idea to wear clothes without sleeves.

   out:
   a. Westerners may wear shorts outside.
   b. Westerners should not wear shorts.
   c. Shorts are not in fashion.

8. (paragraph 6) A tip is expected for the *least* service.

   a. smallest
   b. worst
   c. best

2.10
Application, Critical Evaluation, and Synthesis

1. The people in this reading made the following statements about customs in their own country. Compare each statement with the custom in your country. What would happen if you did (or didn't do) what the person said?

   a. As for gifts, they are not opened when they are given. (paragraph 3).
   b. An invitation for 7 P.M. means you must arrive precisely at 7. (paragraph 4)
   c. There's very little kissing, except between very close relatives, and it's not unusual for sisters to greet each other with a handshake. (paragraph 4)
   d. Chivalry is very much alive, and men open doors of cars and buildings for women. (paragraph 5)
   e. If you admire a possession or an article of clothing,...it is likely to be offered to you....Use discretion about whether to accept the offering. (paragraph 6)

2. Choose two other customs mentioned in this reading and compare them with the customs in your own country.

3. Do you think any of the customs mentioned in this reading from another country would be useful in your country? If yes, why do you think so? If no, why not?

C H A P T E R   T H R E E

The Meeting

R K. Narayan is a famous author from India. This reading comes from his novel *The Vendor of Sweets*, written in 1967. It describes the thoughts of a 60-year-old man, Jagan, who lives in a small city in India. Jagan is remembering how he met his wife in the traditional way many years ago. As this selection begins, Jagan and his brother have just arrived in the village of Kuppam to look at the bride proposed for him by the elders of his family. Excerpted with ellisions and reprinted by permission of Penguin USA and Wallace Literary Agency, Inc.

3.1
First Reading

Read this selection and try to understand the story. Do not worry about understanding every word or detail.

1   Jagan's father had sent his elder son to accompany him and commanded Jagan, "Don't stare at the girl. I have seen her and I know she is good-looking. Don't imagine you are a big judge of persons." At the end of the bumpy journey, he was received with a lot of fuss and seated on a carpet spread on the pyol* of an ancient house. His future father-in-law and a number of his relations had assembled to have a look at the proposed bridegroom and measure him up from different angles. They all engaged him in conversation and tried to judge of his intelligence and outlook. Jagan had already been warned by his elder brother not to be too communicative, as a certain mysteriousness was invaluable in a son-in-law. Everyone kept asking as if in a chorus, "How was your journey?"....

2   Did you have comfortable seats in the train?" asked one examiner sitting at the farthest corner of the pyol; and this time Jagan said on his own, "Of course." It was a matter of propriety to say a good word about the journey when the railway ran over their territory. "What is your subject of study at the college?" asked another one, and Jagan answered, "History," without waiting for his brother's sanction. (Later, when they

---

*pyol** – a room at the front of a traditional house in India

were alone, his brother nudged him and said, "You should have said 'mathematics,' because I know those people would prefer a mathematical son-in-law; all the boys in this part of the country are first-rate mathematicians." To make matters worse, Jagan had not only said, "History," but had also attempted some humorous explanations about his capacity in mathematics). While talking, Jagan cast furtive glances into the hall in the hope of catching a glimpse of his future bride. He had as yet no idea what she would look like. At home he had been shown a rather overtouched shiny photograph of her mounted within a floral border: a sharp-faced young person with tightly braided hair. The photographer had managed to achieve his task without revealing what the girl's eyes looked like, and Jagan, when presented with the photograph, had been unable to scrutinize it for long, because his father was watching him.... She had been decorated with so many ornaments that it was impossible to guess what she really looked like....

3 Now Jagan was going to clear all his doubts; engaged in answering the questions of the assembly, he was seriously wondering when the call would come for him to enter the house and examine his bride. They brought a silver tray heaped with golden-hued jilebi and bonda made of raw banana, and coffee brown and hot, in two silver tumblers, at the sight of which Jagan became hungrier than ever. Left to himself he would have gobbled up the entire lot but a glance from his brother restrained

him.... Even if one was maddeningly hungry one had to say, "Oh, why all this? I cannot eat. We have just had coffee and everything in the train. . ." Jagan mumbled this sentence with the utmost reluctance, jointly with his brother, who uttered it with great clarity. All the same, the code demanded that their hosts should press the delicacies upon them. Then one would have to break off the jilebi minutely with the tip of one's fingers and transfer it to one's mouth, and generally display reluctance or even aversion until pressed again, and then just to please others eat two or three bits in succession and then take an elegant sip of coffee.... Then his future mother-in-law appeared at the doorway, unobtrusively studied the features of her son-in-law, and announced with all gentleness, "Why not adjourn inside?" — addressing no one in particular. Whereupon the master of the house rose to his feet saying, "Why don't you all come in?" which was again a kind of code. Although everyone was fully aware of the purpose of the young man's visit, one had to view the main purpose casually, neither side displaying too much interest or anxiety. Everyone sitting on the pyol got up. Jagan's brother, a born diplomat, was the last but one to respond, and the last was Jagan, though he was burning with impatience....

4   Next they were all led to the central hall of the village home. In honour of this visit many cluttering benches, rolls of bedding, and other odds and ends had been moved to a corner and covered with a huge carpet. On the floor was spread an enormous striped carpet; incense sticks were lit.... For Jagan the scene was heavenly; he felt a momentary satisfaction at the thought that all these preparations were for his sake (even if it was the brother who was the controller). They showed him a seat and the rest arranged themselves around. Jagan kept thinking, "With so many around my view is going to be obstructed and then no one should blame me if I demand a second appearance." There could be no such thing as a second appearance, but his imagination was running wild.... There were stirrings inside, some arguments and protests, and then a little girl with tightly plaited hair emerged grinning with the comment, "Ambika refuses to come out, she feels shy," at which all the elders joked and laughed. The master of the house raised his voice and called, "Ambika, come on, come on, there's nothing to be afraid of in these days." And he addressed the women inside in a general way, "Don't make fun of her, she will be all right. . ." After this preamble a tall girl emerged swishing her lace sari, facing the assembly and smiling, and Jagan's heart gave a thump. "Not at

all like the photo, so tall! I can't believe. . ." The master of the house saved further speculation by announcing, "She is my first daughter," and the tall girl said, "Ambika is coming." The rest Jagan did not hear; he lost interest in the tall girl who was only a sort of advance guard for her younger sister, who came with downcast eyes and bowed head and moved across the arena so fast that Jagan could not take in any detail. "Not short nor tall, nor fat nor puny . . ." Jagan could not arrange her in any clear outline.... "How is she to know what I look like if she flits by so fast?" Jagan speculated. "I don't care what my brother is going to say later; for the present I am going to stare, gaze, and study. I don't care what anybody thinks." He stared unwinkingly at the girl. She had a thick wad of wavy hair, plaited and decorated with flowers, and many pieces of jewellery sparkled on her person.... She shot one lightning glance at him, which somehow, through the fates, coincided with a look he was himself shooting at her, and their eyes met, and Jagan's heart palpitated and raced; and before he could do anything about it, it was all over. The assembly was on its feet, people were leaving, and the vision was gone....

5   When the brothers arrived home..., his mother just smiled at him and asked no questions. His father was drawing water from the well in the back yard; he glanced at Jagan and went on with his work. His sister was circumambulating the sacred tulasi plant in the central yard and grinned at him mischievously, while her lips were muttering prayers. Jagan retired to his room asking himself, "Is no one interested in my opinion of the girl? No one is prepared to inquire whether I like her or not. Does it mean that they are all opposed to the idea?" Nor did his brother pause to enlighten anyone, but proceeded to the back yard in order to help his father at the well.

6   But somehow the information leaked out and his sister was the first to come to his room when he was about to leave for the college, her eyes glittering with mischief. "Aye! Hai!" she cried. "Someone is getting married soon." The house was in great excitement.... Jagan, as became a junior, was careful not to show too much personal interest in his marriage, but he was anxious to know what was going on. He would have been snubbed if he had inquired. He had to depend upon his younger sister, who stood about casually while the elders talked, eaves-dropped, and brought him news. She would seek him out as he sat at his desk apparently studying, and then whisper to him, "Granduncle has approved." "Father is writing to the bride's people tomorrow;

they are waiting for an auspicious time." "Father wants a dowry of five thousand rupees," which really worried Jagan. Suppose the other refused? Then what? "They want to have the marriage celebrated in September." Only three months! Jagan felt scared at the thought of becoming a married man in three months. It was all right as long as one dreamed of a girl and theoretically speculated about marriage, but to become a positive and concrete husband — it was a terrifying reality. "Why do they want to have the marriage so soon?" he asked....

7   One evening the bride's party arrived with huge brass trays covered with betel leaves, fruits, saffron, new clothes, a silver bowl of fragrant sandal paste, a huge heap of sugar crystals on a silver plate, and a pair of silver lamps. A dozen priests were assembled in the hall. A few neighbours and relatives had been invited and Jagan was given a new dhoti* and made to sit in the centre of the assembly. They then unfolded a sheet of paper, on which they had previously spent a considerable time drafting the exact wedding notice, getting the names down correctly. The senior priest of the house, a gaunt old man, stood up and read the notice aloud, his voice quivering with nervousness. It announced that Jagannath, son of so-and-so, was to marry Ambika, daughter of so-and-so, on the tenth of September, etc., etc. The father of the bride handed this important document ceremoniously to Jagan's father, together with an envelope in which he had put currency notes, half the dowry in advance, and gently suggested, "Please ask your elder son to count the cash." Jagan's father made some deprecating sounds but passed the envelope on to his elder son for counting, who lost no time in performing the task and confirming, "Two thousand five hundred."

8   "It was not necessary to count," said Jagan's father gracefully, "but since you insisted on it . . ."

9   "In money matters it is best to be assured. How could I be sure that my counting was perfect? I always like to get cash counted again and again," said Jagan's father-in-law, at which everyone laughed as if it were a brilliant piece of humour. Then they all adjourned for a grand feast prepared by a company of expert cooks. Huge plantain leaves were spread out in the second court, with silver tumblers and bowls for each guest and a dozen delicacies and side dishes in addition to heaps of softly cooked ivory-like rice. A pipe-and-drum party seated in the

---

*dhoti – a long skirt for men that wraps at the waist

front part of the house created enough din to make it known to the whole town that a marriage was being settled. The house had been brilliantly lit with numerous brass lamps as well as gas lamps, which shed an enormous amount of greenish illumination everywhere. Jagan felt overwhelmed by the celebrations. He kept thinking, "All this for my marriage! How seriously they have taken it; no backing out now"....

10 They sent out three thousand invitations. The result was that an enormous crowd turned up by every bus, train, and vehicle at the wedding in Kuppam village.

Reading Times	Reading Speed
1st reading _____ minutes	10 minutes = 198 wpm
3rd reading _____ minutes	9 minutes = 219 wpm
	8 minutes = 247 wpm
	7 minutes = 282 wpm
	6 minutes = 329 wpm

3.2
Second Reading

Go back and read the selection again. Take as much time as you need. Look up some of the unfamiliar words in the glossary at the end of this book or in your dictionary if you wish.

3.3
Third Reading

Read the selection quickly a third time. Concentrate on understanding the main ideas and the meanings of new vocabulary words in the context in which they appear.

3.4
Reader Response

In order to explore your response to this reading, write for 15 minutes about anything that interests you in this selection. You may wish to write about a personal experience this reading reminded you of — or you may wish to agree or disagree with something in the reading. Try to explore *your own thoughts and feelings* as much as possible. Do *not* merely summarize or restate the ideas in the selection.

3.5
Response Sharing

Read your response to two or three other people in your class. Listen carefully to what the others have written. After you have discussed each other's responses, talk about other points of interest in the selection.

3.6
Identifying Main Ideas

Working with the same small group, make a list of the main ideas in this selection. Be sure to state the main ideas in your own words. Don't just copy sentences directly from the text. Think carefully about what the writer is trying to tell you.

3.7
Analyzing the Text

Work with your group members on this exercise. Discuss the answers carefully, particularly if there are disagreements among members of your group. In some cases, there may be more than one possible interpretation.

1. Why did Jagan's brother accompany him?

    a. to make sure Jagan acted properly

    b. to get a second opinion of Ambika

    c. to negotiate the dowry

2. In paragraph 3, the way to eat jilebi and the invitation to come in are referred to as "the code" or "a kind of code." In this paragraph, "code" means:

    a. a way to choose a son-in-law.

    b. secret messages.

    c. the rules for polite behavior.

3. In this reading, Jagan does many things to be polite. Based on this reading, do you think it would probably be polite for Jagan to:

    _____ a. say something complimentary about the village of Kuppam.

    _____ b. take lots of jilebi on his plate and eat them.

    _____ c. not act too interested in the possible bride during the appearance.

_____ d. tell his parents that he was willing to marry Ambika.

_____ e. not ask any questions and let his parents make all the arrangements.

What sections of the reading make you think so?

4. Overall, Jagan seems _____ about the traditional way of meeting a bride in India.

   a. unconcerned   b. pleased   c. dissatisfied

   Why do you think so? Please give examples from the reading.

5. How does Ambika feel about seeing Jagan during the appearance?

   a. She is pleased with Jagan.
   b. She doesn't care one way or the other.
   c. It is not possible to tell from the description.

   Why do you think so? Please give examples from the reading.

3.8
Vocabulary Study

Study the italicized words and phrases in their contexts and guess their meanings. Write your guess on the first line. Then, look up the word or phrase in your dictionary and write the definition on the second line.

1. (paragraph 1) Jagan's father had sent his elder son to accompany him and *commanded* Jagan, "Don't stare at the girl."

   a. (guess) _____

   b. (dictionary) _____

2. (paragraph 2) Jagan, when presented with the photograph, had been unable to *scrutinize* it for long, because his father was watching him.....

   a. (guess) _____

   b. (dictionary) _____

3. (paragraph 3) Although everyone was fully aware of the purpose of the young man's visit, one had to view the main purpose *casually*, neither side displaying too much interest or anxiety.

   a. (guess) _____

   b. (dictionary) _____

4. (paragraph 4) She shot one lightning *glance* at him, which somehow, through the fates, coincided with a look he was himself shooting at her, and their eyes met.

   a. (guess) _____

   b. (dictionary) _____

5. (paragraph 9) "In money matters it is best to be *assured*. How could I be sure that my counting was perfect? I always like to get cash counted again and again," said Jagan's father-in-law.

   a. (guess) _____

   b. (dictionary) _____

3.9
Special Expressions

The phrases in italics have special meaning. Study these phrases in their contexts. Then choose the definition from the list below that means the same thing and write it over the phrase. Check your answers in your glossary or dictionary.

break a promise	laugh at
come into contact	next to last
do right away	now
for (someone's) benefit	observe closely
if (you) could do what	small, unrelated items
(you) want	until now

1. He had *as yet* no idea what she would look like.
2. *Left to himself*, he would have gobbled up the entire lot, but a glance from his brother restrained him.
3. Jagan's brother, a born diplomat, was the *last but one* to respond, and the last was Jagan, although he was burning with impatience.
4. In honour of this visit many cluttering benches, rolls of bedding, and other *odds and ends* had been moved to a corner and covered with a huge carpet.
5. For Jagan the scene was heavenly; he felt a momentary satisfaction at the thought that all these preparations were *for his sake*.
6. "Don't *make fun of* her; she will be all right."

7. [She] came with downcast eyes and bowed head and moved across the arena so fast that Jagan could not *take in* any detail.

8. "I don't care what my brother is going to say; *for the present* I am going to stare, gaze, and study."

9. She shot one lightning glance at him, which somehow, through the fates, coincided with a look he was himself shooting at her, and their eyes *met*.

10. Jagan's father made some deprecating sounds but passed the envelope on to his elder son for counting, who *lost no time* in performing the task and confirming, "Two thousand five hundred."

11. He kept thinking, "All this for my marriage! How seriously they have taken it; no *backing out* now."

3.10
Application, Critical Evaluation, and Synthesis

1. This reading describes how a traditional marriage is arranged in India. Jagan did not see Ambika again until the day of their marriage, and they did not have a chance to be alone together until after the wedding was over. Compare Ambika and Jagan's experience with the way someone in your country typically finds a husband or wife. For example, do parents arrange meetings? How do men and women meet each other? Do people go out on dates before marriage? How important is the approval of parents, grandparents, and other family members? How is the engagement announced? Does the man's or woman's family plan the wedding ceremony and party? Which people (and how many) are invited?

2. In Chapter 2 of this unit, people wrote to advice columns for help with problems. Pretend you are Jagan or Ambika. Write to a columnist, and ask for advice on some aspect of the meeting or the marriage. Then give the columnist's answer based on what you have learned from this reading.

3. How do you think an advice columnist in India would answer any of the problems sent to the Japanese, Chinese, or American columnists in the Chapter 2 reading? As you write your answer, be sure your composition has an introduction, a body, and a conclusion (see page 178 of the Expansion section).

AT THE END OF EVERY UNIT, YOU ARE INVITED TO TURN TO THE EXPANSION SECTION ON PAGE 155. THIS SECTION CONCENTRATES ON SOME OF THE FUNDAMENTALS OF WRITING.

*Kayapó chief recording tribal chants
at the Altamira dam protest.*

Technology: Some Interesting Effects On Our Lives

The twentieth century has been called the century of technology. No matter where we live or what we do, our lives are in some way affected by technology. Some of these effects are good. For example, new medicines and cures for terrible illnesses are discovered every day. We don't have to work as hard because of labor-saving machines. It's much easier to travel and to send and receive information in this age of technology. In this unit, you will read about some unusual applications and unexpected effects of technology.

Discussion

Before you begin reading, think about the following questions and discuss your answers.

1. Make a list of some of the ways that technology affects your daily life (see page 159 for list-making suggestions). Are these good or bad effects? Why?

2. What, in your opinion, is the most important technological development of this century? Why is this development important? How has it changed society? Has this change been good or bad — or a combination of both? Explain.

3. How do you think most people feel about technology? Do they think it is good or bad for themselves and society? Give examples. Are they afraid of technology? Explain and give examples.

4. Do you think television can have negative effects on people? If so, under what conditions? Do you think it is possible to watch too much television? Explain and give examples. Do you think a person could actually become addicted to television, much like one could become addicted to drugs or alcohol?

5. Did you ever have an experience where technology did not have the intended effect, for example, something did not work as it was intended and, therefore, the expected result was different? Explain and give examples.

6. In general, do you think our lives are better or worse because of technology? Do you think technology helps or hinders (hurts) our ability to survive on this planet? Why? Explain and give examples.

The Kayapó chiefs saw the devastation caused by the Tucuri dam—the trees, white and bare, rising ghostlike out of the water.

C H A P T E R   O N E

Technology for the People

Technology is a powerful tool, often controlled by and promoting the interests of huge multi-national corporations and governments. This article, however, is about how other people, ordinary people, around the world have recently been trying to advance their causes and change their lives through the use of sophisticated technology. The information for this article comes from *Discover the World of Science*, *Newsweek*, the *New York Times*, the *Seattle Times*, and National Public Radio.

1.1
First Reading

Read this article quickly for the main ideas. Pay attention to the title and headings and to similarities between the three groups of people discussed in this article. Do *not* stop to look up words in your dictionary.

1 What do the Kayapó Indians in the Amazon and the Runa Indians in the Ecuadorian Andes have in common with students in China? You can't guess? All of these groups have tried to use the latest, state-of-the-art technology to fight for their causes and to gain control over their lives in the last few years.

The Kayapó Indians and Technology

2 The leaders of the Kayapó Indian tribe were alarmed by the damage caused by the Tucurui hydroelectric* dam on the Tocantins River in eastern Brazil. The dam flooded more than 800 square miles of a rain forest, once the home of the Parakanan and Gavioes Indians. The Kayapó chiefs were particularly concerned because Electronorte, a regional power company, was planning to build several dams in the middle of Kayapó territory. One of these dams alone would flood more than 1600 miles of Kayapó land and destroy forever the rich rain forest on this land.

---

*__hydroelectric__ – *hydro* means water. A *hydroelectric dam* makes it possible to use water power to produce electricity.

3   So what did the Kayapó chiefs do? Wearing full ceremonial cos-
    tume, enormous feathered headdresses, and black body paint,
    they paid a visit to the Tucurui dam. In boats, they set out on
    the new lake, and they saw the devastation, the dead trees,
    white and bare, rising ghostlike out of the water. They wanted
    their people to be able to see this great destruction of what had
    once been a beautiful and lush rain forest so that they would
    understand what terrible and irreversible damage a dam would
    do to their own land.

4   But how could they bring their Kayapó tribespeople to the
    Tucurui dam? They couldn't. The dam was too far away from
    Kayapó territory. So they took the Tucurui dam to the people.
    They videotaped it.

5   That was in January, 1989. Within just a few short months,
    hundreds of Kayapó had seen the videotape played on a video-
    cassette recorder powered by a gasoline generator. The
    dramatic film helped unite the Kayapó, who live in villages
    scattered across hundreds of miles of central Brazilian jungle,
    into a powerful political movement. They gathered together to
    demonstrate and protest against the dam construction at one
    of the largest proposed dam sites in their territory. They were
    successful, and for the time being at least, the Altamira dam
    project has been postponed, perhaps for good.

6   What is interesting in this case is that the Kayapó, realizing the
    power of modern technology, have not hesitated to use that
    technology to try to protect their traditional, unmodern life.
    They are fighting to protect their rain forests from destruction
    and, in their case, a picture may indeed be worth many thou-
    sands of words.

The Runa Indians — Land Management By Computer

7   In the Ecuadorian Andes, the Runa Indians are learning land
    management on a 386 AT computer with a 60-megabyte hard
    drive. They started off with a smaller computer system but
    soon outgrew it. They are identifying all the trees in their
    forests and compiling a forest-management inventory, and
    they are also learning to make agricultural spreadsheets to help
    them predict which crops will be the most productive for their
    long-term agricultural purposes.

8   According to Dominique Irvine, a technical consultant who
    works with the Runa Indians, the Runa were not the least bit
    nervous about learning to use the latest computer technology.

They appreciate Western technology and want to use it to advance their own purposes, to gain more control over their own lives, says Irvine. They see Western technology as a useful tool that will help them make better use of their land and resources.

Revolution By Technology In China

9 Meanwhile, in another part of the world, students in China in 1989 tried to create and carry out a pro-democracy revolution by means of facsimile (fax), telephone, photocopier, shortwave radio, wall poster, computer, letter, etc. In other words, the students tried to use every technology available to them to let the outside world know of the bloody massacre carried out by the government troops at Tiananman Square in Beijing and, even more importantly, to relay news about China from the outside world to their fellow Chinese at home.

10 The Chinese government had tried to impose a news blackout in China so that the Chinese people would not find out about the student massacre in Beijing. It did not allow any Chinese television or radio stations to broadcast news of the crisis and the almost 4,000 people who were killed in Tiananman Square when the government cracked down on the students demonstrating for democracy and freedom.

11   But as the Chinese government quickly discovered, it is not so easy to control information now as it once was. For one thing, more than 40,000 Chinese students were attending American universities at that time. Many of them were in daily communication with family and friends in China via telephone, fax, and computer. The students in the United States let people in China know what was going on in China from eyewitness reports on Western television and radio and in newspapers, and they in turn received first-hand news reports from China. These news bulletins from the U.S., complete with the most convincing pictures, sent via fax over the telephone lines, were immediately photocopied and distributed throughout most major Chinese cities.

12   People in China picked up news bulletins over shortwave radio also. About 60 million people usually listen to Voice of America in China. During the student pro-democracy uprising in Beijing, however, VOA began broadcasting more than 11 hours a day in Mandarin (the official language in China), and it has been estimated that VOA reached more than 400 million Chinese. In some cities, courageous people placed radios blasting out VOA news reports high in trees in public parks. When officials confiscated one radio, a new one would begin broadcasting in another area. There was no way the government could control the news in the cities. Former U.S. ambassador to China, Winston Lord, said that as long as there was a single non-government telephone line open between the outside world and China, it would have been impossible for the government to impose a complete news blackout.

Information is Power*

13   Information is power, and whoever controls information has power. Dictators throughout history have understood this concept, and they have usually remained in power as long as they could control information. Now people, ordinary people, want to have information power so that they can control their own destinies. The Kayapó and Runa Indians have both achieved some success in this regard.

Information is Power – In August of 1991, there was a right-wing, reactionary coup by old-line Communists in the Soviet Union. The coup lasted only three days, and one of the reasons that it was not successful was that the leaders did not take over and shut down the country's television, telephones, and other communications with the rest of the world. As John Kohan reported from Moscow, "Tyranny does its best work in the dark, and information is often more powerful than guns." (*Time*, September 2, 1991)

14 Although information is power, information does not automatically bring freedom, at least not immediately. The Chinese students did not succeed in their revolution, perhaps because about 80 percent of the people in China still live in rural areas out of the reach of the students' news bulletins, and the government information blackout worked there.

15 But even though the student revolution did not succeed in 1989 in China, the Chinese students — and people throughout the entire world — learned a powerful lesson: Information technology is not only a powerful tool, it is a powerful weapon in our world today, more powerful in the long run, perhaps, than bombs and other conventional weapons of mass destruction. Ordinary people are beginning to realize these modern-day facts, and they want to control their own destinies by harnessing this technology.

Reading Times	**Reading Speed**
1st reading _____ minutes	8 minutes = 125 wpm
3rd reading _____ minutes	7 minutes = 143 wpm
	6 minutes = 166 wpm
	5 minutes = 200 wpm

1.2
Second Reading

Go back and read the selection again. Take as much time as you need. Look up some of the unfamiliar words in the glossary at the end of this book or in your dictionary if you wish.

1.3
Third Reading

Read the selection quickly a third time. Concentrate on understanding the main ideas and the meanings of new vocabulary words in the context in which they appear.

1.4
Reader Response

In order to explore your response to this reading, write for 15 minutes about anything that interests you in this selection. You may wish to write about a personal experience this reading reminded you of, something you have read or heard about this subject elsewhere — or you may wish to agree or disagree with something in the reading. Try to explore *your own thoughts and feelings* as much as possible. Do *not* merely summarize or restate the ideas in the selection.

1.5
Response Sharing

Read your response to two or three other people in your class. Listen carefully to what the others have written. After you have discussed each other's responses, talk about other points of interest in the selection.

1.6
Identifying Main Ideas

Working with the same small group, make a list of the main ideas in this selection. Be sure to state the main ideas in your own words. Don't just copy sentences directly from the text. Think carefully about what the writer is trying to tell you.

1.7
Analyzing the Text

Work with your group members on this exercise. Discuss the answers carefully, particularly if there are disagreements among members of your group. In some cases, there may be more than one possible interpretation.

1. What are some similarities between the Kayapó Indians in the Amazon, the Runa Indians in the Ecuadorian Andes, and students in China? How are these three groups of people alike? Explain your answer in detail. Give examples.
2. Why were the Kayapó chiefs upset about the Tucurui hydroelectric dam which, after all, was not even on their land?
3. Explain why the Runa Indians are using computer technology. What are some of their objectives (things they want to accomplish)?

4. The Chinese students did not succeed in their pro-democracy revolution. But according to this article, they did succeed in something. What did they succeed in? Explain and give examples.

5. Explain the meaning of the title, "Technology for the People"? Does this title fit the article? Explain.

1.8
Vocabulary Study

Study the italicized words and phrases in their contexts and guess their meanings. Write your guess on the first line. Then, look up the word or phrase in your dictionary and write the definition on the second line.

1. (paragraph 2) The leaders of the Kayapó Indian tribe *were alarmed* by the damage caused by the Tucurui hydroelectric dam on the Tocantins River in eastern Brazil.

   a. (guess) _____

   b. (dictionary) _____

2. (paragraph 3) In boats, they set out on the new lake, and they saw the *devastation*, the dead trees … rising out of the water. They wanted their people to be able to see this great destruction of what had once been a beautiful … rain forest.

   a. (guess) _____

   b. (dictionary) _____

3. (paragraph 5) The dramatic film helped *unite* the Kayapó, who live in villages scattered across hundreds of miles of central Brazilian jungle, into a powerful political movement.

   a. (guess) _____

   b. (dictionary) _____

4. (paragraph 10) The Chinese government had tried *to impose* a news blackout in China so that the Chinese people would not find out about the student massacre in Beijing.

   a. (guess) _____

   b. (dictionary) _____

5. (paragraph 13) Now people, ordinary people, want to have information power so that they can control their own *destinies*.

   a. (guess) _____

   b. (dictionary) _____

1.9
Cloze Exercise

Choose the correct word for each blank. Discuss your choices with your group.

The twentieth century is often _____ the age of

(1) call – called

technology. We are all _____ by technology in our

(2) effected – affected

daily _____. Let's look at television, for example. Many

(3) lives – lifes

studies _____ shown that our ideas about

(4) has – have – had

_____ world events are shaped by what we have

(5) importants – important

_____ on television. If we have seen a lot about

(6) see – saw – seen

_____ event, we get the idea that _____ event

(7) a – an   (8) a – an – this

is more important than an event we _____ not seen

(9) has – have – had

or heard that much about. For good or for bad, television clearly

_____ the way we see reality.

(10) influence – influences – influenced

1.10
Application, Critical Evaluation, and Synthesis

1. Go back to the discussion questions at the beginning of the unit. Discuss question 3 using information from this article as well as information from other sources.

2. Imagine that you are a consultant and you have been hired by the Kayapó Indians to advise them on other steps they could take to protect their rain forest. How would you advise them to inform other people of the problem? How can they again use technology for their own purposes? Write a letter to the Kayapó tribal council with your proposals.

3. The situation the Kayapó Indians face brings up an interesting and complex problem. They are trying to save a precious natural resource, their rain forest, from destruction by a hydroelectric dam. On the other hand, however, hundreds of thousands of people would benefit from the electricity generated by the dam. What factors should the government consider in making its decision about whose interests to protect? Why is this a complicated problem?

4. Have you ever seen a news event portrayed on television that you knew was not true or not exactly as presented? What was the situation? How was it portrayed? How was the real situation distorted? Why was it distorted? How did you know it was distorted? What was your connection to the situation? Begin with freewriting on this topic to explore your ideas (see page 161 for instructions on freewriting). If you wish, do a second freewriting (see page 162 for instructions).

5. Aldous Huxley *(Brave New World)* and George Orwell *(1984)* were two important twentieth century writers who both warned about the danger that technology would be used to control people's minds. They feared that governments would use technology to take away freedom of choice and liberty, to turn people into obedient robots who would not question the state. What do you think about their fears? Do you think governments use technology to control what people think? How does the information in this article agree or disagree with Huxley's and Orwell's ideas? Explain and give specific examples.

How Viewers Grow Addicted to Television

Some people become addicted to television, just as others become addicted to alcohol or drugs according to results of several recent studies. What is television addiction, and how does it affect its victims? Daniel Goleman discusses these questions in an article that appeared in the *New York Times* (Oct. 16, 1990). Excerpted and reprinted by permission.

2.1
First Reading

Read this selection quickly for the main ideas. Pay attention to the titles and headings as you read. Do *not* stop to look up words in your dictionary.

1 The proposition that television can be addictive is proving to be more than a glib metaphor. The most intensive scientific studies of people's viewing habits are finding that for the most frequent viewers, watching television has many of the marks of a dependency like alcoholism or other addictions.

2 For instance, compulsive viewers turn to television for solace when they feel distressed, rather than only watching favorite programs for pleasure. And though they get temporary emotional relief while watching, they end up feeling worse afterward.

3 For a decade or more, researchers have pursued the hypothesis that some television viewers are addicted to watching. But only this year have a handful of studies produced the strongest evidence yet that some compulsive viewers are indeed addicted under standard diagnostic criteria.

What Is Television Addiction?

4 There is no definition of television addiction on which all researchers agree. But people who call themselves "television addicts," studies find, watch television twice as much as the average viewer. One study found that self-described addicts

watched an average of 56 hours a week; the A.C. Nielsen Company reports the average for adults is just above 30 hours a week.

5 Recent studies have found that two to twelve percent of viewers see themselves as addicted to television; they feel unhappy watching as much as they do, yet seem powerless to stop themselves.

6 Portraits of those who admit to being television addicts are emerging from the research. For instance, a study of 491 men and women reported this year by Robin Smith Jacobvitz of the University of New Mexico offers these character sketches.

7 A 32-year-old police officer has three sets in his home. Although he is married with two children and has a full-time job, he manages to watch 71 hours of television a week. He says, "I rarely go out anymore."

8 A 33-year-old woman who has three children, is divorced and has no job, reports watching television 69 hours a week. She says, "Television can easily become like a companion if you're not careful."

9 A housewife who is 50, with no children, watches 90 hours of television a week. She says, "I'm home almost every day and my TV is my way of enjoying my day."

Insights On Normal Viewing

10 The studies also shed new light on more ordinary viewing habits, showing that people who are emotionally dependent on television simply represent extremes of behavior seen from time to time in most viewers.

11 In a study comparing television viewing with leisure activities like sports, reading, or gardening, television fared poorly as a diversion. While ordinary viewers say television relaxes them while they watch, afterward they feel far less relaxed, less happy and less able to concentrate than after participating in sports or other leisure activities . ...

Measuring Television Addiction

12 The most commonly used scale to measure television addiction includes using television as a sedative, even though it does not bring satisfaction; lacking selectivity in viewing; feeling a loss of control while viewing; feeling angry with oneself for watching so much, not being able to quit watching and feeling miserable when kept from watching it.

13 "They turn on the TV when they feel sad, lonely, upset, or worried, and they need to distract themselves from their troubles," said Robert McIlwraith, a psychologist at the University of Manitoba. Dr. McIlwraith reported his findings on television addiction at the annual meeting of the American Psychological Association in Boston last August [1990].

14 The reported television watching data is from studies done between 1976 and 1988 on several different groups involving close to 1,200 men and women who volunteered to fill out questionnaires about their activities and moods whenever they were alerted by beepers they carried.

15 In analyzing the data for people's television-watching habits, Robert Kubey, a psychologist now at the School of Communications at Rutgers University, worked with Mihaly Csikszentmihalyi, a psychologist at the University of Chicago.

16 Their findings are reported in *Television and the Quality of Life*, published this year [1990] by Lawrence Erlbaum Associates. While their conclusions are drawn from the studies involving

more than a thousand people, the most detailed results come from a study in which 107 men and women reported on their experiences at randomly selected moments throughout the day for a week.

17 The third of the men and women in the smaller study who watched television the most were markedly different from the rest of those studied. As a group, the compulsive watchers were more irritable, tense, and sad than the others, and felt they had little control over their lives.

18 For most people, there was a strong relationship between being in a bad mood and watching television to get out of it. The strongest pattern predicting that people would watch television in the evening was that in the morning they felt the day was going badly, and by the afternoon they were in a bad mood....

19 "It's common for people to say they are selective television watchers," said Dr. Kubey. "They'll say they sat down just to watch 'L.A. Law,' but they're still watching three hours later. A great many people feel powerless to get up and turn it off." ... The longer [compulsive viewers] watch, the more passive and less discriminating they become, Dr. Kubey found.

20 Oddly, while most people said they were more relaxed while watching television than they had been before starting, they ended up feeling far less relaxed once they stopped. "We found no evidence that television offers emotional rewards that extend beyond viewing," Dr. Kubey said.

21 Moreover, the longer people watch television, the less rewarding they find it, the intensive study of 107 people showed. These experiences with television were strongest among the compulsive viewers. Not only did they report feeling worse than most people as they watched television, but their spirits drooped all the more once they stopped watching. What little lift they get from television, though, is enough in many cases for most frequent viewers to become dependent on it, Dr. Kubey said....

22 [Compulsive viewers feel] uncomfortable when they are alone with nothing to do, the study showed. For such people, idle time is unpleasant, making them all the more ready to seek solace from television.... Television addicts were far more likely to say they watched TV when feeling lonely, sad, anxious or angry, and to use it to distract themselves from things that bothered them or when they were bored....

Reading Times	**Reading Speed**
1st reading _____ minutes	7 minutes = 153 wpm
3rd reading _____ minutes	6 minutes = 177 wpm
	5 minutes = 214 wpm
	4 minutes = 267 wpm

2.2
Second Reading

Go back and read the selection again. Take as much time as you need. Look up some of the unfamiliar words in the glossary at the end of this book or in your dictionary if you wish.

2.3
Third Reading

Read the selection quickly a third time. Concentrate on understanding the main ideas and the meanings of new vocabulary words in the context in which they appear.

2.4
Reader Response

In order to explore your response to this reading, write for 15 minutes about anything that interests you in this selection. You may wish to write about a personal experience this reading reminded you of, something you have read or heard about this subject elsewhere — or you may wish to agree or disagree with something in the reading. Try to explore *your own thoughts and feelings* as much as possible. Do *not* merely summarize or restate the ideas in the selection.

2.5
Response Sharing

Read your response to two or three other people in your class. Listen carefully to what the others have written. After you have discussed each other's responses, talk about other points of interest in the selection.

2.6
Identifying Main Ideas

Working with the same small group, make a list of the main ideas in this selection. Be sure to state the main ideas in your own words. Don't just copy sentences directly from the text. Think carefully about what the writer is trying to tell you.

2.7
Analyzing the Text

Work with your group members on this exercise. Discuss the answers carefully, particularly if there are disagreements among members of your group. In some cases, there may be more than one possible interpretation.

1. Make a list of words and phrases that you associate with *addiction*, e.g., out of control, drugs. Discuss your list with your group members.
2. Make a list of some of the symptoms (signs) of television addiction. Discuss your list with your group members and give an example of each point on your list.
3. What are some ways that the viewing habits of a television addict differ from those of a normal viewer?
4. Write whether these statements are true (**T**) or false (**F**).

   a. _____ Television addicts say that they feel better after watching TV for long periods of time.

   b. _____ Television addicts watch about the same amount of TV as normal viewers do.

   c. _____ Television addicts have trouble controlling the amount of television they watch and the programs they watch.

   d. _____ Television has a long-term relaxing effect on viewers, particularly heavy viewers.

   e. _____ Television addicts tend to turn to TV as a means of solace and comfort when they feel sad or depressed.

5. Look at the character sketches of the three television addicts (paragraphs 7–9). What generalizations (general comments) could you make about these three TV addicts?

2.8
Vocabulary Study

Study the italicized words and phrases in their contexts and guess their meanings. Write your guess on the first line. Then, look up the word or phrase in your dictionary and write the definition on the second line.

1. (paragraph 1) Television can be *addictive*...Watching television has many of the marks of a dependency like alcoholism or other addictions.

    a. (guess) _____

    b. (dictionary) _____

2. (paragraph 2) Compulsive viewers turn to television for *solace* when they feel distressed, rather than only watching favorite programs for pleasure.

    a. (guess) _____

    b. (dictionary) _____

3. (paragraph 6) Portraits of those who admit to being television addicts *are emerging* from the research.

    a. (guess) _____

    b. (dictionary) _____

4. (paragraph 17) As a group, the compulsive viewers were more irritable, *tense*, and sad than the others, and felt they had little control over their lives.

    a. (guess) _____

    b. (dictionary) _____

5. (paragraph 20) *Oddly*, while most people said they were more relaxed while watching television than they had been before starting, they ended up feeling far less relaxed once they stopped.

    a. (guess) _____

    b. (dictionary) _____

2.9
Cloze Exercise

Choose the correct word for each blank. Discuss your choices with your group.

What about _____ television shows
(1) childrens – childrens' – children's

like "Sesame Street"*? What do children _____
(2) learn – learns – learned

from them? How do _____ shows affect children?
(3) this – that – these

On _____ positive side, studies show that children
(4) a – an – the

_____ watch "Sesame Street" regularly learn
(5) who – which – that

_____ colors, letters, and numbers earlier
(6) there – their – they're

_____ children who do not watch the show. However,
(7) then – than

_____ the negative side, some _____
(8) in – on – at   (9) study – studies

show that regular "Sesame Street" viewers _____
(10) has – have – had

some problems in school later on. They _____
(11) has – have – had

trouble concentrating and focusing _____
(12) there – their – they're

attention in a regular classroom setting. Some of them

_____ less imagination and fantasy
(13) show – shows – showed

_____ their classmates. They may be more passive, less
(14) then – than

creative, and less able to handle _____ –solving
(15) problem – problems

activities. Thus, the report card for "Sesame Street" is mixed — good

marks in some areas and bad marks in others.

---

*"Sesame Street" is the name of a children's educational television show that is made in the United States but shown in many countries around the world.

2.10
Application, Critical Evaluation, and Synthesis

1. Rate yourself on the television-watching assessment below (1 = no, not at all, never; 2 = somewhat, very little, occasionally; 3 = yes, usually, a lot, more than average; 4 = definitely, a great deal, very often, very much)

   a. Watching television is one of my
      favorite activities.   1   2   3   4

   b. I use television as an escape from
      my worries and concerns.   1   2   3   4

   c. I find it difficult to stop watching
      TV once I start.   1   2   3   4

   d. I am very selective about what I
      watch.   1   2   3   4

   e. I get most of my information about
      world news from TV.   1   2   3   4

   f. Watching TV relaxes me and makes
      me feel better about life in general.   1   2   3   4

   g. I would rather watch TV than go out
      with my friends.   1   2   3   4

   h. Television is like a companion for me.   1   2   3   4

   i. I usually agree with what I see on TV.   1   2   3   4

   j. My TV viewing time a week is
      (1) 10 or fewer hours
      (2) 11 to 30 hours
      (3) 30 to 50 hours
      (4) More than 50 hours   1   2   3   4

Scoring — Add up your scores for *a, b, c, g, h, j*.

   6 – 12 You are definitely not a TV addict.
   13 – 16 You are in the average range.
   17 – 20 You are on the high side of average. You may have a TV
            problem. Watch it!
   21 – 24 You need some TV therapy fast!

---

*Note: This is an informal survey, and it has not been validated.

2. Television has many positive features not mentioned in this article. What are the most worthwhile shows on television in your opinion? Describe these shows and explain why you think they are worth watching. Make a chart like this one to help you organize your ideas.

TELEVISION SHOWS		
Worthwhile TV Shows	**Good Qualities**	**Effects on Viewers**

3. Do you know a TV addict (according to the symptoms described in this article)? Who is this person? Describe this person's TV watching habits and their effects on her or him.

4. Keep a TV log for a week. Every day write down what you watched that day, for how long, your mood (how you felt) before you started watching, while you were watching, and when you finished. Look over your log at the end of the week. What does it tell you about yourself? Are you satisifed with your TV watching habits? Are there any habits you might want to change? Which ones? Why?

5. Did you ever see something on TV that had a very powerful effect on you and made you completely change your mind about a subject? What was the subject or issue? What did you see that changed your mind? Begin by freewriting (see page 161 for instructions on freewriting). Do a second freewriting if you wish (see page 162). Follow instructions for developing your freewriting into a composition (page 178).

Sorry, Wrong Number!

Technology affects us — even when it does not work as intended. Jorge Miguel Aviles, a Venezuelan filmmaker, gives an account of how the telephone system shaped his life in unexpected ways in the first piece. The second selection is a personal reflection on the powerful effect of television on the life of a young girl. It was written by a young Latina actress/writer who calls herself "Domenica." She is now living and working in New York City. Both reprinted by permission.

3.1
First Reading

Read these two selections quickly for the main ideas. Think about similarities and differences between the two pieces. Do *not* stop to look up words in your dictionary.

1 It was 1967. I was young, just 21, and I was trying to start a small business in Caracas. At that time in my life, I still believed that everything was possible. It was rough going in the beginning (and, as it turned out finally, in the middle and at the end), but I was hopeful that, against all odds, I would succeed and become a successful man at an early age.

2 My business, which shall go nameless (and could have been anything), depended heavily upon telephone contacts. I had to telephone offices all over Caracas and, by hook or by crook, convince people to let me get a foot in their door to talk to them about my services. As a rule, they remained singularly unimpressed by my overtures, and I had to resort to a variety of dramatic and highly-imaginative tactics to accomplish my mission: to get in the door so that I would have the opportunity to stage another dramatic performance. I believed I would be irresistible in person. I was 21 at the time ....

3 At any rate, it was essential, a *sine qua non**, that my telephone, my sole means of contact with my would-be clients, be in

---

*sine qua non – a Latin phrase meaning essential, absolutely necessary (literally, "without which nothing").

perfect working order. In the beginning, the telephone did my bidding, and my lack of initial success could not be attributed to the telephone company. However, one day, just when the first dark traces of desperation were beginning to emerge around the corners of my mind, I began to encounter unusual communication experiences. I began to enter a sort of twilight zone.

4 This is what happened. I was calling an office for the third time, one of the few offices where they had not outright rejected my overtures. I had detected the slightest hesitation on their part, a possible weakness in their defenses against me and my kind, in a previous call, and I was eager to press my luck. I placed my call and then I waited as it rang once, twice, three times.

5 A woman's voice answered on the third ring (good luck, I thought to myself!) and before she could defend herself, I seized the moment and took the electronic stage to deliver my charming and persuasive speech. It was a monologue, carefully rehearsed dozens of times before the mirror in my aunt's bathroom (I was already subconsciously thinking of video

telephones, you see). I refused to allow my audience any openings. Finally, however, I paused for dramatic effect — to breathe, actually — and the voice said, "I am very sorry but you have the wrong number. This is not an office. It is a private residence."

6 I apologized profusely and hung up. Recovering myself somewhat, I tried the number again, this time exercising the greatest care in placing my call. No matter! The same voice answered. I apologized again. She graciously accepted. The same thing happened a third time, a fourth time ... . By then the lady, very charming, even greeted me by name.

7 I contacted the telephone service company and pleaded my desperate case before them. They assured me that it was only a minor problem (how they ascertained this, I have no idea, but at that time, even major corporations were extremely optimistic) and that it would be taken care of immediately.

8 Just after I had finished this call, my telephone rang. My first return call from a potential client! All of my boldness and suave composure vanished. My nerves were suddenly ajangle. I had my first case of stage fright. I thought of not answering and simply bolting from my office (a bedroom in my aunt's house). But somehow I marshalled up all my courage and managed to answer on the third ring (for luck) in my deepest, most professional voice. Unfortunately, my voice cracked ever so slightly as I announced the impressive name of my enterprise.

9 It was the lady's voice again. This time it was her turn to apologize, and my turn to graciously and charmingly accept. We laughed together over our crossed wire relationship. A few minutes later, she telephoned back. Again apologies, this time a few jokes. She had a lovely voice, the sort of voice that a singer or an actress might have....

10 By the time the telephone company finally repaired my line, I had sent a huge bouquet of flowers to the lady with my card. She had called to thank me, very easy with our telephone lines joined. One thing led to another .... Six months later, the gracious lady and I eloped. We pooled all of our resources and flew off to Mexico City to start a new life together, leaving family and friends — and my strange and pathetic little business — far, far behind.

11 Unfortunately, it was not an entirely happy ending. Yes, we were madly in love with each other. That was never the question. But after a few years the realities of our life together could not match our powerful dreams and so, with great reluctance and sadness, we separated. We were brought together by illusions and separated by realities.

12 Years later, I was back in Caracas making a political documentary film, and I was invited to the opening of a new art gallery. Just as I was turning away from a conversation with one of the artists whose work was on display, I heard again the voice, that unmistakable voice. And yes, there she was, beautiful and charming as ever. She introduced me to her husband, a well-known and prosperous Argentinian industrialist whom I immediately recognized from pictures in the media.

13 "Whenever you are in Caracas," her husband said, "you must call us." We all laughed and then she went back to her life, and I went back to mine.

Now go on to the second piece by Domenica, the young Latina actress/writer.

Television Lights Up My Life

1 We each have a photograph album in our minds with snapshots of special moments in our lives — moments of delight, of happiness, of joy — and even if we are sitting in a dark room, we can call up these precious images from the past whenever we want, and we will see that scene again with the same sharp clarity. The face of a special friend or lover, the moment of joy when we learned we received a special prize or award, the family gathered together, little ones grinning in front, older ones more serious and somber in the back. Yes, these are the special moments, captured forever in our minds, that we can call up at will.

2 But, wait, there are other moments preserved forever in our minds, moments that stand out with the same clarity, the sharp lines and colors never fading through the years. These are painful moments, moments when we confronted a terrible truth, a truth that would change our lives forever whether we wanted it to or not. And they too are carefully tucked away and preserved in our photograph album.

3 I remember such a moment now. I was nine years old and I tiptoed quietly into our neighbors' yard one evening with my sisters to sneak a look at their television through the open window. I had never seen this wonderful, magical box before — it was the first and only television in our tiny village at that time — and I stared in awe (and some fright) at a beautiful lady inside the box who was speaking a strange language (English, it turned out to be) and cooking an egg. I could see that she was very rich, maybe a queen or a princess. And then a gentleman came in. He said, "Hi" (one of the few English words I understood). He was also very rich. Maybe he was a king. They were laughing together, and he kissed her, right there in the Santiagos' house! We gasped in delicious shock.

4 Suddenly the Santiagos' maid, an ax-faced young girl of 14 from the mountains, appeared like an evil spirit at the window and saw us standing there with her beady little eyes.

5 "What is it, Rosita? Is something out there?" called Mrs. Santiago from inside the darkened room.

6 "No, it's nothing," said Rosita, "Only some dirty little pigs and chickens" and she spit at us as she slowly closed the shutters in our faces.

7 In that moment, in those few seconds as Rosita closed us out, I saw myself illuminated in the ghostly light of the television, flickering from within. I saw my faded and torn pink dress, a cast-off from an older sister, until then my favorite sister and my favorite dress. I saw my scratched, dirt-stained legs, my bare feet. I saw my long, tangled hair. I saw big, frightened black eyes burning in a dark, little face.

8 My sisters were laughing and giggling hysterically as we scrambled, truly like wild pigs and chickens, out of the Santiagos' yard. "Hurry!" they called to me, "Before they throw cold water on us!"

9 They were laughing. But I was crying. Why? Because, in the flickering light of the television, I had seen a truth, a painful truth — that I was poor, that I was not as good as others, that I was condemned in some horrible way. And, for the first time, I knew shame. I was ashamed of myself and of my life. — I never forgot that moment of painful, burning truth. When I was just 15 years old, I ran away from my family, from my village, even from my country, and I never went back again.

10 Yes, television changed my life completely in just a single flash. Television destroyed me, my life — and from the broken pieces, I made a new life. This is one of the painful pictures in the photograph album of my mind.

Reading Times	Reading Speed
1st reading _____ minutes	10 minutes = 154 wpm
3rd reading _____ minutes	9 minutes = 171 wpm
	8 minutes = 192 wpm
	7 minutes = 220 wpm

3.2
Second Reading

Go back and read the selections again. Take as much time as you need. Look up some of the unfamiliar words in the glossary at the end of this book or in your dictionary if you wish.

3.3
Third Reading

Read the selections quickly a third time. Concentrate on understanding the main ideas and the meanings of new vocabulary words in the context in which they appear. Think again about the similarities and differences between the two pieces.

3.4
Reader Response

In order to explore your response to these readings, write for 15 minutes about anything that interests you in these selections. You may wish to write about a personal experience these pieces reminded you of — or you may wish to agree or disagree with something in one or both of the readings. Try to explore *your own thoughts and feelings* as much as possible. Do *not* merely summarize or restate the ideas in the selections.

3.5
Response Sharing

Read your response to two or three other people in your class. Listen carefully to what the others have written. After you have discussed each other's responses, talk about other points of interest in the selections.

3.6
Identifying Main Ideas

Working with the same small group, make a list of the main ideas in these selections. Be sure to state the main ideas in your own words. Don't just copy sentences directly from the text. Think carefully about what the writers are trying to tell you.

3.7
Analyzing the Text

Work with your group members on this exercise. Discuss the answers carefully, particularly if there are disagreements among members of your group. In some cases, there may be more than one possible interpretation.

1. What ideas do you have about Jorge Miguel Aviles, the writer of the first selection? What kind of person do you think he is? What are some characteristics of his personality? Why do you suppose he and

his wife separated if they were so much in love with each other? What do you think he meant when he said, "We were brought together by illusions and separated by realities"?

2. By the same token, what is your impression of the writer of the second selection, Domenica? How would you describe her character? Do you think she is a strong person? A proud person? Why was this such an important experience in her life?

3. These two selections have some common features. In what ways are these selections similar?

4. These selections also have clear differences. What are some of the differences? Does one selection appeal to you more? Which one? Why?

5. Tone (the feeling and emotion of a selection) is very important in both of these selections. How would you compare the tone of these two selections?

3.8
Vocabulary Study

Study the italicized words and phrases in their contexts and guess their meanings. Write your guess on the first line. Then, look up the word or phrase in your dictionary and write the definition on the second line.

1. (paragraph 2) I had to [try anyway I could] to get in the door so that I would have the opportunity to stage another dramatic performance. I believed I would be *irresistible* in person. I was 21 at the time …

   a. (guess) _____

   b. (dictionary) _____

2. (paragraph 11) Unfortunately, because this was real life and not a *novel*, the story does not have an entirely happy ending.

   a. (guess) _____

   b. (dictionary) _____

3. (paragraph 11) We were madly in love with each other. … But after a few years the realities of our life together could not match the powerful dreams…. We were brought together by *illusions* and separated by realities.

   a. (guess) _____

   b. (dictionary) _____

4. ("Television Lights Up My Life," paragraph 1) We each have a photograph *album* in our minds with snapshots of special moments in our lives ... and even if we are sitting in a dark room ... we can see that scene again with the same sharp clarity.

   a. (guess) _____

   b. (dictionary) _____

5. (paragraph 7) I saw my faded and torn dress, a *cast-off* from an older sister, until then my favorite sister and my favorite dress.

   a. (guess) _____

   b. (dictionary) _____

3.9
Cloze Exercise

Choose the correct word for each blank. Discuss your choices with your group.

Life is a great teacher it _____ been said many

(1) has – have – had

times, and I am sure we can all _____ of many

(2) think – thinks

situations when we _____ important and powerful

(3) learn – learned

_____ from life. Domenica, for example,

(4) lesson – lessons

_____ class differences that were so

(5) confront – confronts – confronted

_____ that she had to change _____

(6) painful – painfuls   (7) his – her – the

life completely. Her sisters, for some reason, did not

_____ the same lesson and this

(8) learn – learns – learned

_____ up an interesting question.

(9) bring – brings – brought

Why _____ we learn what we do? Why

(10) do – does – did

_____ some people _____ by

(11) do – did – are   (12) affected – effected

an experience and _____ are not? What are some of the
(13) *other – others*

_____ for these individual _____
(14) *reason – reasons*   (15) *difference – differences*

among people? These are important questions and, so far, we do not
have all the answers to them.

3.10
Application, Critical Evaluation, and Synthesis

1. Both of the selections in this chapter focus on experiences that
    transformed (changed) the life of the writer. Have you ever had a
    transforming experience, an experience that changed your life so
    much that you were, in effect, a new or different person afterwards?
    What was the experience? How did it change your life? Was it a
    good or bad change? Do you regret this change? Did you learn
    something from this experience? If so, explain.

2. In the first selection, the writer talks about meeting someone acci-
    dentally. As we know, this accidental meeting had a great effect on
    his life (his personal life and perhaps his professional life). Did you
    ever accidentally meet someone who became important to you in
    some way and, in effect, changed the course of your life? If so, who
    was the person? Explain the situation and what happened.

3. Many people believe in destiny or fate. In other words, they believe
    that nothing happens accidentally or by chance, that everything is
    destined to happen as it does. What do you think? Explain and give
    examples if you can.

4. In the second selection, Domenica describes the moment in which
    she became aware of poverty. Do you remember the moment when
    you as a child became aware of class (social and economic) differ-
    ences — that some people had more and others had less? Why do
    you think Domenica may have connected her poverty with a sense
    of worthlessness (not being as good as other people)?

5. Have you ever compared your life to the lives of people you see on
    television? Do you think that making such comparisons could have
    bad (even perhaps dangerous) effects on some people? If so, explain
    and give examples. In general, the world presented on most TV pro-
    grams is quite a lot different from the world most of us live in. Do you
    think this gap is important or significant in any way? Please explain.

*AT THE END OF EVERY UNIT, YOU ARE INVITED TO TURN TO THE
EXPANSION SECTION ON PAGE 155. THIS SECTION CONCENTRATES
ON SOME OF THE FUNDAMENTALS OF WRITING.*

Photographs help us remember special moments in the past.

How to Improve Your Memory

P eople often say, "Oh, I have a terrible memory. I can't remember a thing." Of course, they are wrong. If they really couldn't remember a thing, they wouldn't be able to remember the words to tell you they couldn't remember. Whatever we say or do involves some degree of memory. Without memory, we would not be able to get up, get dressed, prepare our breakfast, let alone speak and respond to others.

Memory is one of the most important components of learning because learning involves storage of information, among other things. Scientists are constantly studying how the memory works and trying to find reasons for why we remember some things and forget others. Why is it, for example, that many old people remember the distant past clearly and distinctly, but they cannot recall what they did earlier that day? Why do most of us have trouble remembering names? How is it possible that some people are able to remember long lists of words or numbers with ease?

Discussion

Before you begin reading, think about the following questions and discuss your answers.

1. Do you have trouble remembering names? Have you ever felt embarrassed or uncomfortable because you could not remember someone's name? Explain.
2. If you have something important to remember, how do you try to remember it? Do you have any special plan or strategy for remembering information?
3. Describe your study habits. How do you study in order to remember and use information at a later date? What is the best way to study if you want to understand a subject well?

4. Do you frequently lose or misplace important things — keys, your wallet or pocketbook, your passport? Why do you think you lose these things?

5. Have you ever seen or heard of a person with an unusual memory, someone who could remember a great number of words or numbers with ease? How do you think these memory experts are able to perform these difficult tasks?

6. Did you ever experience "déjà vu" — the strong feeling that you are reliving an experience, i.e., you see something for the first time but you are sure you have seen it in exactly the same way before, that you have had that exact experience before? Explain.

"I'm So Sorry but I Can't Remember Your Name"

"I'm so sorry but I can't remember your name. I'm no good at names." These are familiar words to all of us. How many times have you said this or heard someone else say it? Most of us spend a great deal of time apologizing for not being able to remember someone's name and sometimes we even warn people when we meet them that we are not going to remember their name later: "Don't expect me to remember your name. I'm just terrible on names!" Obviously it would be much more convenient for all of us if we could remember names and, as a matter of fact, there are ways we can improve our memory for names. All it takes is a little concentration and practice. Here is some practical advice on how to remember names.

1.1
First Reading

Read this passage quickly for the main ideas. Pay attention to the headings. Do *not* stop to look up words in your dictionary.

I'm Sorry But I'm Terrible With Names

1   You're with a friend. You're walking down the street one bright, sunny day and suddenly you see an old teacher, someone you had liked and admired very much when you had been in her class a few years before. You rush across the street, you greet her warmly, and you start to introduce your friend to your teacher. . . and suddenly you cannot remember your teacher's name. Then, to make matters worse, you become so excited and flustered that you forget your friend's name in your panic. The result? You mumble an apology, you try to laugh about it, but you feel like a fool. "I am terrible with names," you explain.

2   You are not alone. Embarrassing moments like this have happened to all of us at one time or another. For no apparent reason,

our mind suddenly goes blank, and we cannot remember names, or familiar telephone numbers, or where we have put our keys. Sometimes it is just a minor inconvenience, but other times the consequences are very serious indeed.

Encoding Information Carefully

3   Why do we remember and why do we forget? These two questions are at the heart of the psychology of learning, and scientists have carried out countless experiments over the years to investigate these questions.

4   And what have scientists discovered about memory? First of all, the way we encode information (put information into our brain) at the beginning affects our ability to remember the information later. All of us have our own special memory system built into our brains. If we want to remember new information, we have to be able to fit the new information into our memory system if we want to be able to retrieve, to get to and use that information later. Let's suppose you are in your living room and you are trying to decide where to put a new sweater. Well, if you want to find this sweater easily and quickly later when you need it, you would probably put it in the drawer in the bedroom with your other sweaters. Another person, however, might put the sweater in a closet near the door so that it would be easy to get to before going outside. Sweaters and remembering information may seem pretty far apart, but they both require storage, preferably in a logical place that you can get to quickly and conveniently later.

Five Easy Steps To Remembering Names

5   Back to names. Let's suppose you, like most of us, think you have a terrible memory for names. You regret it, you apologize for it, but deep down, you believe there is nothing you can do about it. You were just born that way. But is this, in fact, true? No. You can, if you want, improve your memory for names easily and dramatically if you follow a few simple rules:

a.   *Pay close attention when you are being introduced to someone.*

This point sounds so simple and so obvious, something that anyone would know, but as a matter of fact, most of us do *not* pay close attention during an introduction. We immediately start thinking about how we are not going to remember the name. Essentially, we are too busy programming ourselves for failure to pay attention. How exactly do you pay close attention? **Look directly at the person (in a friendly way, of course) and, at the same time, listen carefully to his or her name.**

b. *Repeat the name and make a comment or ask the person a question about his or her name.*

◆ *Louise Montag.* Are you by any chance related to Jacqueline Montag?

◆ *Bekaert.* How do you spell your name? What is the origin of your name?

◆ *Dominique LeBlanc.* What a beautiful name. Are you French?

Don't worry. You won't offend the person. Research shows that people feel closely connected to their names and they like the attention they get if you show interest in their name. They feel flattered and see the attention as a compliment to them. And you get to practice saying their name aloud while looking at them, associating the name with the face in your mind.

c. *Associate the name with something (or someone) familiar to you.*

Try to form a picture to connect the name with in your mind. For example, if the name is Elizabeth, you might visualize Queen Elizabeth in your mind. If the name is Carpenter, think of a carpenter sawing a piece of wood or pounding a nail into the wall. **If you cannot think of a mental picture, maybe you can associate by sound**, e.g. the name Kaoru, you might associate with "car", the name Keri with the verb "to carry" (and you could imagine this person carrying something to reinforce your sight-sound associations).

Try to find something in your mind to attach this name to, just as you might hang a coat on a peg or a hook. Once you have the name "pegged" or "hooked", you have succeeded in attaching the name to your memory system and it won't get lost so easily.

d. *Use the person's name from time to time in conversation.*

Practice strengthens the memory and will help you remember the name longer. Think of practice as cutting a path through the jungle of your mind. The more you use the path after you cut it, the more marked it will be and the easier it will be to find and use this path when you need it. By the same token, the more you practice the name, the easier it will be for you to recall it when you need or want to.

e. *Try to recall the person's name and face soon after your meeting.* Later the same day, review the person's name and face in your mind. This review can take only a few seconds, but it helps strengthen the memory. This practice keeps the memory path open in your mind.

Memory Wizards: What is the Secret Of Their Magic?

6   Some people are able to remember a phenomenal number of names. They meet a group of people once and, six months later, they can recall each person's name instantly when they meet again. This is obviously a very useful skill for business, politics or, for that matter, any field in life. After all, we all love to be remembered, to stand out for other people. We cannot help but be flattered that we made such a strong impression on someone else and that they still remember us so clearly.

7   The secret of remembering names is not really mysterious or magical. All you have to do is follow these few simple rules outlined above carefully, and you too can become a name wizard. You will be able to store a great number of names efficiently and conveniently in your mind and get them out quickly when you need them. Try it. You'll be amazed at how easy it is!

Reading Times		**Reading Speed**
1st reading _____ minutes		7 minutes = 143 wpm
3rd reading _____ minutes		6 minutes = 167 wpm
		5 minutes = 200 wpm
		4 minutes = 250 wpm

1.2
Second Reading

Go back and read the selection again. Take as much time as you need. Review the five steps carefully. Look up some of the unfamiliar words in the glossary at the end of this book or in your dictionary if you wish.

1.3
Third Reading

Read the selection quickly a third time. Concentrate on understanding the main ideas and the meanings of new vocabulary words in the context in which they appear.

1.4
Reader Response

In order to explore your response to this reading, write for 15 minutes about anything that interests you in this selection. You may wish to write about a personal experience this reading reminded you of, something you have read or heard about this subject elsewhere — or you may wish to agree or disagree with something in the reading. Try to explore *your own thoughts and feelings* as much as possible. Do *not* merely summarize or restate the ideas in the selection.

1.5
Response Sharing

Read your response to two or three other people in your class. Listen carefully to what the others have written. After you have discussed each other's responses, talk about other points of interest in the selection.

1.6
Identifying Main Ideas

Working with the same small group, make a list of the main ideas in this selection. Be sure to state the main ideas in your own words. Don't just copy sentences directly from the text. Think carefully about what the writer is trying to tell you.

1.7
Analyzing the Text

Work with your group members on this exercise. Discuss the answers carefully, particularly if there are disagreements among members of your group. In some cases, there may be more than one possible interpretation.

1. Make a list of why people frequently forget names, according to this passage (see page 159 for list-making suggestions). Where does the memory problem start? Explain.

2. Why are these statements obviously not true: "I can't remember a thing. I have no memory at all."

3. Put these five steps to remembering names in order.

    _____ a.   Associate the name with something (or someone) familiar to you.

    _____ b.   Use the person's name from time to time in conversation.

    _____ c.   Pay close attention when you are being introduced to someone. Listen carefully.

    _____ d.   Try to recall the person's name and face soon after the first meeting.

    _____ e.   Make a comment or ask the person a question about his or her name.

4. Explain the meaning of each of these five steps in detail. Give examples.

5. The writer comments that practice is like making a path through a jungle. What does she mean? Explain this analogy*.

1.8
Vocabulary Study

Study the italicized words and phrases in their contexts and guess their meanings. Write your guess on the first line. Then, look up the word or phrase in your dictionary and write the definition on the second line.

---

*analogy – Comparing two objects or ideas. Saying these two things are alike in some way or aspect: "Her lips were like a rose." Analogies are frequently used in poetry.

1. (paragraph 2) Embarrassing moments like this have happened to all of us at one time or another. For no apparent reason, our mind suddenly *goes blank*, and we cannot remember names, or familiar telephone numbers, or where we have put our keys.

   a. (guess) _____

   b. (dictionary) _____

2. (paragraph 4) All of us have our own special memory system built into our brains. If we want to remember new information, we have to be able to fit the new information into our memory system if we want to be able to *retrieve*, to get to and use that information later.

   a. (guess) _____

   b. (dictionary) _____

3. (paragraph 5 b) Don't worry. You won't *offend* the person [by commenting on their name or asking a question about their name]. Research shows that people feel closely connected to their names and they like the attention they get if you show interest in their name.

   a. (guess) _____

   b. (dictionary) _____

4. (paragraph 5 c) Try to form a picture to connect the name with in your mind. For example, if the name is Elizabeth, you might *visualize* Queen Elizabeth in your mind.

   a. (guess) _____

   b. (dictionary) _____

5. (paragraph 5 d) Think of practice as cutting a path through the jungle of your mind. The more you use the path after you cut it, the more marked it will be and the easier it will be to find and use this path when you need it. *By the same token*, the more you practice the name, the easier it will be for you to recall it when you need or want to.

   a. (guess) _____

   b. (dictionary) _____

1.9
Cloze Exercise

Choose the correct word for each blank. Discuss your choices with your group.

Would you like to be a better student? It's not hard if you learn

how to _____ your study habits. If
　　　　　(1) improve – improving – improved

_____ have a chapter to read, _____
(2) I – you – we – she　　　　　　　　　　　　　*(3) watch – see – look*

at the title and section headings first. Look at the illustrations. Try to

predict _____ this chapter will probably be
　　　　　(4) that – if – what – why

about. Then read through the chapter _____ just to
　　　　　　　　　　　　　　　　　　　(5) quick – fast – quickly

get the main ideas. Go back and read slowly and _____
　　　　　　　　　　　　　　　　　　　　　　　(6) careful – carefully

the second time. Spend extra time on the difficult _____
　　　　　　　　　　　　　　　　　　　　　　　(7) part – parts

trying to figure them out. Look up _____ words
　　　　　　　　　　　　　　　(8) unfamiliar – unfamiliars

and try to understand them as they are _____ in the
　　　　　　　　　　　　　　　　　　　　(9) use – using – used

chapter. After that, read through a third _____. Try to read
(10) time – times

quickly this time. If the chapter contains a _____ of new
(11) lots – lot

information, do not hesitate to read it through a fourth or fifth time even.

Finally, look at all the section _____ and try to
(12) heading – headings

reconstruct the information in each section in your own words. Think of

your own _____ to support important points in
(13) example – examples

the chapter. Review the chapter again in a few days — or

_____. Then, if you have an exam over this chapter,
(14) week – weeks

you will not need to cram everything in the night _____.
(15) before – after

You will be able to recall the information with ease because you took

time to study it properly in the beginning.

1.10
Application, Critical Evaluation, and Synthesis

1. Go back to the discussion questions at the beginning of the unit.
    Discuss the first question in detail.
2. Most of us do not study as effectively as we could. On a scale of 1 to 5
    (with 1 being low or very bad), how would you rate your study habits?
    Explain and give examples. How could you improve your study
    habits? Refer to **1.9** in answering these questions if you wish.
3. What did you learn about remembering names from this article?
    Which point (or points) made the strongest impression on you? Why?
4. How do polite introductions take place in your culture? Do you
    shake hands with each other? Bow? Do you look the other person
    directly in the eye? Why? Or why not? What do you say when you
    are introduced to someone?
5. Do you have any special memory scheme (plan or strategy) for
    remembering names? If so, please explain in detail and give examples.

CHAPTER TWO

I've Been Here Before

Have you ever had the strange feeling that you are reliving an experience you have had before? You say to yourself, "I know I have been here and done this same thing before in exactly the same way." You can't remember where or when — but you know you are reliving an experience you've had before. In this article, you will read about some explanations for this curious phenomenon and some other interesting facts about brain and memory as well.

2.1
First Reading

Read this passage quickly for the main ideas. Pay attention to the headings. Do *not* stop to look up words in your dictionary.

1   You've been invited to a party by a friend of a friend. You're feeling a little nervous because you won't know many people at this party. However, you decide to accept. You go to a house where you've never been before. Your host greets you warmly at the door and welcomes you to his home. You walk into a large room full of people — and suddenly you have the eerie feeling that you have been here before, that you have walked into this same room and that you have seen these same people standing in the same small groups chatting with each other. You feel frightened by this odd, spooky feeling. What's going on? Calm down. What you are experiencing is **déjà vu** — which, in French, means "already seen." Your mind has just played a harmless little trick on you, and it's nothing to worry about.

Am I Reliving Something from a Former Life?

2   People sometimes say that déjà vu is evidence of a former life and that the reason you feel you are reliving an experience is

because, in fact, you had that same experience in a former life. What a fascinating idea! But it's probably not the case. Psychologists have offered a number of explanations for the curious phenomenon of déjà vu. One theory is that it helps you confront and overcome anxiety: You're not nervous about going into a party where you know hardly anyone because you've done it before (or your brain tricks you into thinking you've done it before) — so you can relax. After all, if you've done it before, it's not so threatening, and you can do it again. Another theory is that you are experiencing **recognition disorder;** your brain tricks you into believing that a similar experience is, in fact, the very same experience.

3 William Braud, a psychologist at the Mind Science Foundation in San Antonio, Texas, offers two other possible explanations. It may be that an electrical current is accidentally generated in the area of your brain associated with memory and familiarity. Electrical activity in this area just *makes you feel as though* you're reliving or reexperiencing something all over again. No matter where you are or what you are doing at the time, you will have the sensation that you are repeating something you have done before, and everything will seem strangely familiar to you.

4 Braud's second explanation is that the two sides of your brain are experiencing a very slight time lapse. In this case, the right side of your brain experiences something just a fraction of a second before the left side experiences it. Therefore, the left side is tricked into thinking that this has happened before, a long time before — not just a fraction of a second before. Whatever the explanation for déjà vu, you should know that it is a common phenomenon — roughly, two-thirds of adults experience it at some point in their lives — and it's not dangerous.

I Know You But I Can't Remember Your Name

5 You've had the experience of meeting someone at school or in the street and not being able to think of the person's name. This is a common occurrence, and it's an example of a failure in **retrieval search**. Your brain is not able to find the clues it needs to unlock your memory. We've all had the experience of putting our keys somewhere and not being able to find them later. In this case, our brain cannot find a memory we have put somewhere.

6   A failure in retrieval can be explained by environmental factors — what is going on around you. For example, you may have been distracted when you were originally introduced to the person, so you didn't really learn the name very well in the beginning. The memory loss many older people experience can often be explained by problems in the encoding stage.

7   Why is this? The reason is if several things are going on simultaneously when they are trying to learn something new, it is especially distracting for older people. They'll have more trouble recalling this information later on than younger people will. However, it is interesting to note that older people recall information in distracting circumstances just as quickly and as well as younger people do. So part of the answer for older people is to cut down distractions in the encoding stage.

8   Can you improve your memory for names? The answer is yes. Here are some suggestions:

   • When you're introduced to someone, pay attention. Listen carefully to the person's name, look at the person carefully, and then say the name out loud.
   • Try to connect the person's name and face and link them with a picture in your mind. If the person's name is Rose, you can picture her holding a beautiful rose.
   • Repeat the person's name aloud to yourself several times later on — and try to recall the person's face as you repeat the name.

These encoding suggestions will help you in your retrieval searches in the future. Remember: The key to retrieval is careful encoding.

Why Did I Open the Refrigerator?

9   You hurry into the kitchen, open the refrigerator door, and suddenly you draw a blank. "What am I looking for?" you ask yourself. "What am I doing here?" Don't worry. You're not losing your mind. We've all had this kind of memory lapse. The explanation is simple. If you think about something very quickly, it goes into your short-term memory — and it goes right back out in just a few seconds. You have not transferred the information from short-term to long-term memory, so you won't be able to retrieve it later on.

"Why did I come into the kitchen?"

10 What can you do to help you recover your missing short-term memory? One suggestion is that you go back to where you were before you forgot. Put yourself back in the original context. So, for example, if you were sitting in a chair listening to music in the living room, go back into the living room. The chances are the context will help you remember, and when you are back in the living room, you will suddenly think, "Oh, yes, I was thirsty and I wanted something cold to drink, and that's why I went to the refrigerator." If for some reason you can't go back to where you were before, try retracing your steps in your mind. Think back to the context you were in before, and this may jog your memory.

In 1492, Columbus Sailed the Ocean Blue

11 One way to try to remember facts or dates is to make a rhyme and include the information you want to remember: "In **1492**, Columbus sailed the ocean **blue**." "Thirty days has **September**, April, June and **November**. . ." If you can remember the first line of the rhyme, the chances are you can remember the whole thing because the second line has to rhyme with the first, and that limits the possibilities.

It's Like Riding a Bike

12   Once you learn how to ride a bike, you will always remember how to do it. People say this all the time and, in fact, there is a lot of truth in it. The reason is that a memory of this type is a **kinesthetic memory**, and it involves the muscular system. Kinesthetic memories are closer to instinct than other memories are, and they may be linked with survival. Braud, at the Mind Science Foundation, has suggested that kinesthetic memories are so strong because they are motor actions, and they have been given more memory wiring (electrical pathways) in the brain.

That Was Our Song

13   You hear a song that was popular years ago when you were in high school and suddenly you travel through time and space and you are back there. "This reminds me of when I was 17 and I was in love with so-and-so. That was our song. . ." and for the next few minutes, you are lost in memory. So long ago but it could have been yesterday. The reason? Music can trigger whole memories for us. We remember not only the words of the song, but the whole context of where we were when that song was playing at an important moment in our past. It all comes back in a powerful rush of memory.

14   Smells can summon up the past as well. You may smell something cooking — and suddenly you think of your Aunt Sophie, who used to bake a plum cake that smelled just like that 20 years ago. Or you smell wood burning — and you remember a camping trip when you were ten and sitting with friends around the camp fire. Again, smells, like music, can evoke a whole context of memory for us years and years after the fact, and these memories give a rich texture to our present lives.

Reading Times	Reading Speed
1st reading _____ minutes	9 minutes = 143 wpm
3rd reading _____ minutes	8 minutes = 161 wpm
	7 minutes = 174 wpm
	6 minutes = 215 wpm

2.2
Second Reading

Go back and read the selection again. Take as much time as you need. Look up some of the unfamiliar words in the glossary at the end of this book or in your dictionary if you wish.

2.3
Third Reading

Read the selection quickly a third time. Concentrate on understanding the main ideas and the meanings of new vocabulary words in the context in which they appear.

2.4
Reader Response

In order to explore your response to this reading, write for 15 minutes about anything that interests you in this selection. You may wish to write about a personal experience this reading reminded you of, something you have read or heard about this subject elsewhere — or you may wish to agree or disagree with something in the reading. Try to explore *your own thoughts and feelings* as much as possible. Do *not* merely summarize or restate the ideas in the selection.

2.5
Response Sharing

Read your response to two or three other people in your class. Listen carefully to what the others have written. After you have discussed each other's responses, talk about other points of interest in the selection.

2.6
Identifying Main Ideas

Working with the same small group, make a list of the main ideas in this selection. Be sure to state the main ideas in your own words. Don't just copy sentences directly from the text. Think carefully about what the writer is trying to tell you.

2.7
Analyzing the Text

Work with your group members on this exercise. Discuss the answers carefully, particularly if there are disagreements among members of your group. In some cases, there may be more than one possible interpretation.

1. What does the term **déjà vu** mean? What are some of the explanations for this phenomenon?

2. Read each statement carefully. Then, write whether these statements are true (**T**) or false (**F**).

    a. _____ Déjà vu is evidence of a former life, according to this article.

    b. _____ Older people have more trouble than younger people encoding information when there are distractions around them.

    c. _____ Older people have more trouble than younger people recalling or retrieving information when there are distractions around them.

    d. _____ If you cannot remember why you went into the kitchen, it is a long-term memory problem.

    e. _____ Rhymes can help people remember facts.

3. When you cannot remember why you went into the kitchen, what are two things you can do to help you remember?

4. What is **kinesthetic memory**? Why is it likely to be stronger than other kinds of memories? Give some examples of kinesthetic memories.

5. Why can a smell make you remember something from your childhood? Explain how smell is related to memory. Give examples.

2.8
Vocabulary Study

Study the italicized words and phrases in their contexts and guess their meanings. Write your guess on the first line. Then, look up the word or phrase in your dictionary and write the definition on the second line.

1. and **2.** (paragraph 1) Suddenly you have the *eerie* feeling that you have been here before, that you have walked into this same room and that you have seen these same people standing in the same small groups chatting with each other. You feel frightened by this odd, *spooky* feeling.

eerie

a. (guess) _____

b. (dictionary) _____

spooky

a. (guess) _____

b. (dictionary) _____

3. (paragraph 13) Music can *trigger* whole memories for us. We remember not only the words of the song, but the whole context of where we were when that song was playing at an important moment in our past.

trigger

a. (guess) _____

b. (dictionary) _____

4. and **5.** (paragraph 14) Smells can *summon* up the past as well. Smells, like music, can *evoke* a whole context of memory for us years and years after the fact.

summon

a. (guess) _____

b. (dictionary) _____

evoke

a. (guess) _____

b. (dictionary) _____

2.9
Cloze Exercise

Choose the correct word for each blank. Discuss your choices with your group.

How _____ the memory work?
(1) do – does – did

_____ is an important question for scientists.
(2) This – That – These

They _____ that the memory actually
(3) think – thinks – thought

_____ two important components: short-term
(4) involve – involves

and long- _____ memory. All kinds of
(5) term – terms

_____ come into our short-term memory
(6) information – informations

all the _____ . Only part of _____
(7) time – times   *(8) this – that – these*

information gets into our long-term memory, where

_____ is more or less permanently
(9) he – she – it – they

_____ for later use.
(10) store – storing – stored

2.10
Application, Critical Evaluation, and Synthesis

1. Have you ever experienced déjà vu? Explain in detail.
2. Older people frequently have trouble getting information from short-term memory into long-term memory so that they can get to and use the memory later. Have you met an older person who has some kind of memory problem? Describe the problem and give examples. How would you explain this problem according to information given in this article? What can be done to help older people with this problem?

3. Do you have favorite songs that remind you of important experiences or periods in the past (for example, when you were in high school, your first boyfriend or girlfriend)? What are these songs and what are the feelings they awake in you when you hear them? How does this article explain the connection between certain pieces of music and feelings?

4. Do you have things you always forget to do, no matter how hard you try to remember them? What are these things? Why do you think you forget them? Is there a reason for your forgetting?

5. Are there particular smells or aromas that are connected with certain memories for you? Describe and explain. According to this article, why have you made these connections? Explain the importance of environment and context in memory.

C H A P T E R   T H R E E

How to... uh... Remember!

G ordon H. Bower is well known for his work in the psychology of learning, particularly in the area of memory and how it affects learning. Bower believes, on the basis of his research, that memory is a skill that can be taught and that people can learn how to use their memory more effectively if they learn certain strategies. In the article below, Bower shows how one kind of mnemonic (memory) strategy can be used to improve memory. He goes on to note later in the article (not reprinted here) that there are many mnemonic strategies in addition to this one that can help us organize information more efficiently and effectively in memory. Excerpted and reprinted with permission from *Psychology Today*. Copyright © 1973 (P.T. Partners, L.P.).

3.1
First Reading

Read this article quickly for the main ideas. Pay attention to the headings and phrases printed in boldface. Do *not* stop to look up words in your dictionary.

The Method Of Loci

1   ... A second **mnemonic*** for learning lists of items is the method of **loci ("locations")**: it works by relating the items... to a standard list of known locations. One of the first references to this mnemonic system was made by Cicero, who tells the story of a man named Simonides. While attending a large banquet, Simonides was called outside and during his absence the roof of the hall collapsed, killing all of the revelers. The bodies of the victims were so mangled that they could not be identified by their relatives. Simonides, however, was able to identify each of the corpses by recalling where each person sat before the tragedy. He did this by visualizing the room and mentally walking about, "seeing" who had been seated in each chair.

---

*mnemonic – a memory strategy that helps you remember something by associating it with another object and visualization (making a mental picture of what you are trying to remember connected with the associated object.)

Make a mental picture to help you remember the items you need at the store.

This feat so impressed him that he came to believe that all memory worked by placing objects or ideas into definite locations. The mnemonic is known as the method of loci because it depends on putting items to be remembered into a series of "locations."

How To Use the Method Of Loci

2   To use the method of loci, you must first establish a list of "memory snapshots" of locations taken from along a familiar route, such as a walk through your house. (A building, campus, or city would serve as well.) You must be able to see clearly and to recite the different distinctive locations on your list. To learn any new list of items you simply take a "mental walk" through your list of loci, placing successive items in your imagination at successive locations along your familiar route. You should connect the items to their locations by visualizing some vivid interaction between the item and the things at a given location.

3   When you need to recall the items, you simply take another mental walk along your familiar route and see what items have been placed there. For example, suppose that you need to buy many items at the grocery store, including milk, bread, and bananas as the first three. The first three snapshots of your pre-memorized list of locations might be your front hallway closet, the kitchen refrigerator, and your favorite easy chair. To learn the first three items of your shopping list, you should visualize a vivid image of quarts of milk stacked up and bursting in your hallway closet, then a dagger-like loaf of bread piercing the refrigerator door, and then large bunches of bananas piled up in your easy chair.

4   A long list of items to be learned would require a long list of familiar locations in memory. As each object to be learned is studied, it is placed in imagination at the next location on your list of familiar loci. You should try to visualize a clear mental picture of the object "doing something interesting" at the location where it is placed. Later, in the grocery store, you can recall your shopping list by an imaginary walk through your house, pausing to "look at" what you've placed earlier at the standard locations in your route.

5   This system provides a series of memory hooks on which you can snag items and keep them from getting away. The number of loci can be expanded indefinitely according to one's needs. The system does more than just connect an item to something that is already known. It provides a series of permanent hooks or memory pegs **to which you already have reliable access.**** Since the peg-list doesn't change, the pegs provide cues that can stimulate recall of the needed items.

Experimental Evidence That Loci Improves Memory

6   A man who developed the method of loci to a fine art was the subject of Alexander R. Luria's book, *The Mind of a Mnemonist*. Known simply as "S," this man performed remarkable feats of memory, recalling long lists of words without effort, and often retaining material many years.

**to which you already have reliable access – information which is already clearly in your memory such as, for example, the location of all of the rooms in your house. The "hooks" or "pegs" would be these rooms in your house.

7   There is also experimental evidence that the method of loci improves memory. Sometimes subjects who use this system are able to recall two to four times as much material as control subjects. In a study by John Ross and Kerry A. Lawrence, students studied a list of 40 nouns using the loci method. Immediately after each student studied the list, he tried to recall it in correct order. The next day the subject returned and again recalled the list before learning a new list of 40 items. Each student learned several lists this way. The average recall of words studied a day before was 34 out of 40 in correct order. This performance is vastly superior to that of students who used **rote-learning** techniques.***

Shopping With Mnemonics

8   In a direct comparison of the methods, David Winzenz and I had college students study five successive "shopping lists" of 20 unrelated words. They were allowed five seconds to study each word; they tried to recall each list immediately after studying it, and at the end of the session they tried to recall all five lists (100 items). Some subjects learned [the lists] using the loci mnemonic or slight variations on it, while our control subjects were left to learn by their own devices (which typically consisted of rote rehearsal).

9   The subjects using the loci mnemonic recalled the words far better than the controls on both the immediate test and the end-of-session test. At this end-of-session test, the mnemonic subjects remembered an average of 72 items out of 100, whereas the controls remembered only 28. Furthermore the items recalled by subjects using the mnemonic were usually assigned to the right position on the right list, whereas the control subjects were very poor at remembering the position and list of the few scattered items they did recall.

***rote-learning** – Trying to memorize something by repeating it over and over but not associating the items or trying to visualize them as in mnemonics. Rote rehearsal is the most common memory strategy and the least effective one because the items are not "hooked" or "pegged" in memory.

Reading Times	Reading Speed
1st reading _____ minutes	8 minutes = 163 wpm
3rd reading _____ minutes	7 minutes = 186 wpm
	6 minutes = 217 wpm
	5 minutes = 266 wpm

3.2
Second Reading

Go back and read the selection again. Take as much time as you need this time. Look up some of the unfamiliar words in the glossary at the end of this book or in your dictionary if you wish.

3.3
Third Reading

Read the selection quickly a third time. Concentrate on understanding the main ideas and the meanings of new vocabulary words in the context in which they appear. You may wish to read this article a fourth and perhaps a fifth time due to the technical nature of some of the material.

3.4
Reader Response

In order to explore your response to this selection, write for 15 minutes about anything that interests you in this article. You may wish to write about a personal experience this selection reminded you of, something you have read or heard about this subject elsewhere — or you may wish to agree or disagree with something in the selection. Try to explore *your own thoughts and feelings* as much as possible. Do *not* merely summarize or restate the ideas in the selection.

3.5
Response Sharing

Read your response to two or three other people in your class. Listen carefully to what the others have written. After you have discussed each other's responses, talk about other points of interest in the selection.

3.6
Identifying Main Ideas

Working with the same small group, make a list of the main ideas in this selection. Be sure to state the main ideas in your own words. Don't just copy sentences directly from the text. Think carefully about what the writer is trying to tell you.

3.7
Analyzing the Text

Work with your group members on this exercise. Discuss the answers carefully, particularly if there are disagreements among members of your group. In some cases, there may be more than one possible interpretation.

1. Who was Simonides? What kind of memory feat did he perform? Explain in detail.
2. What is the **mnemonic of loci**? Explain how it works and why it is effective.
3. What is the difference between **rote rehearsal** and the **mnemonic of loci**? Which is more effective for long-term recall? Why? What is the chief defect or problem with rote rehearsal?
4. Explain what "pegs" and "hooks" are. Why are they important in mnemonics?
5. According to research results cited here, does loci improve memory? Explain in as much detail as possible.

3.8
Vocabulary Study

Study the italicized words and phrases in their contexts and guess their meanings. Write your guess on the first line. Then, look up the word or phrase in your dictionary and write the definition on the second line.

1., 2., and 3.   (paragraph 1) While attending a large banquet, Simonides was called outside and during his absence the roof of the building collapsed, killing all of the *revelers*. The bodies of the victims were so *mangled* that they could not be identified by their relatives. Simonides, however, was able to identify each of the *corpses* by recalling where each person sat before the tragedy.

revelers

a. (guess) _____

b. (dictionary) _____

mangled

a. (guess) _____

b. (dictionary) _____

corpses

a. (guess) _____

b. (dictionary) _____

4.   (paragraph 5) [The system of loci] provides a series of memory hooks on which you can *snag* items and keep them from getting away.

a. (guess) _____

b. (dictionary) _____

5.   (paragraph 7) The average recall of words studied a day before was 34 out of 40 in correct order. This performance is *vastly* superior to that of students who used [other memory strategies].

a. (guess) _____

b. (dictionary) _____

3.9
Cloze Exercise

You are ready for a new challenge. This time *you* supply an appropriate word for each blank instead of choosing from a list as you have done before. Discuss your word choice with your group. *Note*: In some cases, more than one word may be appropriate, or no word may be needed.

How _____ we get information from

_____-term memory to long-term memory so that we
(2)

can _____ the information later when we need or
(3)

_____ to? _____ of all, we have to pay
(4)   (5)

_____ attention to whatever we are _____
(6)   (7)

to learn or remember. We have to _____ or associate
(8)

what we want to remember _____ something we already
(9)

_____ in our minds. After we have made this association,
(10)

we _____ to rehearse. This _____ that
(11)   (12)

we _____ practice recalling the information. The best
(13)

way to rehearse _____ to combine the new information
(14)

_____ something we already know; for example, we
(15)

can make up _____ own examples to support a
(16)

point _____ want to remember. If we do not
(17)

_____ up our own associations, we will not be able to
(18)

remember the information as _____ or as long because
(19)

memory is _____ active, creative process.
(20)

3.10
Application, Critical Evaluation, and Synthesis

1. Make a list of ten unrelated words. Using the system of loci described in this chapter, memorize these words in order. Have one of your classmates check your list as you try to recite the words in order. How many did you get right? If you made mistakes, why do you think you made these mistakes?

2. Try to recite your list after 24 hours. How many words did you get right this time? Remember: you have to recite your words in order.

3. Now memorize a new list of ten words. Follow the same instructions given in questions 1 and 2 above.

4. Now try to recite your first list. How many did you get right this time? Did the loci system help you improve your memory? Explain and give examples.

5. "Memory is an active, creative process." What does this statement mean? Do a short freewriting to explore your ideas on this subject (see page 161 for freewriting instructions). After you have done your freewriting, write a second draft. This time, explain your points and give examples. Finally, what did you learn about memory and how it works from this unit?

AT THE END OF EVERY UNIT, YOU ARE INVITED TO TURN TO THE EXPANSION SECTION ON PAGE 155. THIS SECTION CONCENTRATES ON SOME OF THE FUNDAMENTALS OF WRITING.

Developing Research and Writing Skills

When you finish each unit, you should turn to this section if you want to work more on writing and learn how to do basic library research for a research paper. We suggest that you read through this entire section first to give yourself an overview. After that, you should refer to various topics as needed. For example, you will probably need to review the Getting Started section and the Library Research topic several times before you understand all of the points mentioned. You may need several study sessions to learn the uses of direct quotation and paraphrasing and the differences between them. Finally, use this section as a resource manual; refer to various parts of it from time to time to help you learn how to do process writing, basic library research, and write research papers.

CONTENTS

4.1
Choosing a Writing Topic

At the end of every chapter, we give you ideas for topics you could write about. These are only suggestions, and you may wish to make up your own writing topics from time to time. Your teacher and/or your group members may help you select a topic sometimes. We suggest that you try if possible to choose or make up a topic that is interesting to you because it will be easier for you to write about something you are interested in.

4.2
Getting Started

Once you have chosen a topic, you obviously have to get started writing. Getting started is the hardest part of writing for most people. However, there are ways of making this task easier, and we would like to introduce you to some of these techniques at this time.

We suggest that you try all of the techniques a few times until you find the one or ones that help you the most. All of these techniques are useful, but you may find one of them works better than another for helping you develop ideas on a certain topic.

1. Brainstorming

Brainstorming helps you get ideas for your writing project. Here is how you do it. First, you take a pen or pencil and a piece of paper (scrap paper is fine for this task) and write your topic on your paper. Read your topic over a few times to yourself. Then let your mind wander. Write down any words or phrases that come to your mind in connection with your topic. Here's an example. Let's suppose your general topic is fashion and you want to write about blue jeans. First, write your topic on your paper as we suggested. And then jot down (write down quickly) any ideas that come to mind related to your topic.

blue jeans	*youth/young people*
clothing	*freedom*
comfortable	*enjoyment*
casual	*leisure*
informal	*recreation*

Brainstorming with other people: This is an excellent group activity if you are working with others on developing a writing or discussion project. How do you brainstorm with a group? First, choose one person to be the group recorder. This person will be in charge of writing down any words or phrases group members suggest. This can be done on paper or on a blackboard or a flip-chart.

Making connections: After you brainstorm, the next step is to make connections between your ideas. Look at your list. Ask yourself (or your group members, if you are working with a group) these questions:

a. Is anything on this list related to anything else on this list? If yes, draw a line between these ideas to connect them.

⎧ *comfortable*	⎧ *enjoyment*
⎨ *casual*	⎨ *leisure*
⎩ *informal*	⎩ *recreation*

b. As you are making connections, do you suddenly think of something new, something that you didn't have on your list? Good! Write it in now anywhere on your list. Read over the items on your list several times and see if there are any more additions you want to make.

c. Is there anything you want to leave out? Is there something on your list that you now think is not really closely related to your topic? What do you do? Cross it out. Read over your list again and cross out any other items that are not interesting to you or are not closely related to your topic.

d. Can you put your ideas in an order? Write "1" by the idea you want to write about first, "2" by the idea you want to write about second, etc.

 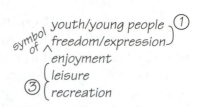

Making a list

We have mentioned making a list above, but in fact, there are several ways to make a list as you are brainstorming. One technique is not necessarily better than another, but one may prove to be more useful to you under certain circumstances. Again, we suggest you experiment with different techniques.

Here is an example of the most common listing technique. The writer is listing the advantages and disadvantages of wearing uniforms to school.

WEARING UNIFORMS IN SCHOOL

Advantages	**Disadvantages**
• looks neat	• everyone looks the same
• identifies students with school	• can't express personality & style
• no difference between rich and poor students	• discourages creativity and individuality
• less expensive for parents to buy clothes	• creates a dull group mentality
• students can concentrate on school better (?)	• interferes with freedom of expression
• makes a better public impression	• discourages independence and decision-making
• creates a serious atmosphere	

A list of this kind is especially useful for exploring issues where you are trying to look at two sides of a subject, for example, the advantages and disadvantages of something, reasons for doing something, and reasons for not doing something.

Mapping and clustering

Another useful listing technique is mapping or clustering. Instead of making a linear list as illustrated above, you start by writing your topic in the center of your page in a box. And then as you brainstorm for ideas, you write your ideas around the topic. As you write one idea down, you may think of another idea related to it, so you could write this second idea close to the first idea in a *cluster* (a group of ideas).

Here is an example of a map with some clusters. The topic is earrings and it is written in the box in the middle of the page.

Mapping and clustering can be useful for helping you see relationships between ideas.

Mapping can be very useful for showing important events or ideas in relation to each other. In the example below, a student has drawn a map of her life. We can easily see the high points and the low points of her life from this map; also we can see which events stand out in some way for her because she has circled them.

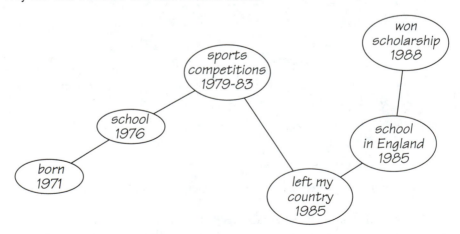

If you are telling a story or recounting an experience, mapping can help you organize the material in order. Additionally, it will help you see which events are the most important ones and thus need to be emphasized in the telling or writing.

It doesn't matter what form your brainstorming takes — linear lists, mapping, clustering — and it doesn't matter what you make your notes on — a clean piece of paper, the back of an old envelope, a paper napkin, any kind of scrap paper. This is just an activity for your eyes only — to help you explore your own thoughts and feelings relating to the topic as the first step in writing about the topic.

2. Freewriting

Another way to get started and to explore your ideas on a topic is to do some freewriting at the beginning. You can do freewriting after or in place of brainstorming.

How do you freewrite? You write for 10-15 minutes about your topic. *You should write anything that comes into your mind. If nothing comes into your mind, just write "I can't think of anything" but keep on writing. Don't stop writing. Keep your pen or pencil moving across your paper for the entire time.*

When you are freewriting, don't think about grammar, spelling, or punctuation. Just write! And don't stop writing until your time is up.

After you finish, read over what you have written. Draw a line under anything that seems interesting to you — a sentence or two, maybe just a phrase. You can freewrite again beginning with this *kernel* (the part you underlined). You can continue to freewrite several times. Each time you freewrite, you bring your ideas on your topic more and more into focus.

Here is an example of freewriting. The writer (Deidre) is freewriting on the topic of jewelry. After she finished, she underlined the part she thought was most important and interesting to her (the kernel). (*Note:* Grammar and spelling have not been corrected.)

Jewelry. I like to wear jewelry especialy earrings, I have a favorite pair of earrings and I usually wear them. I dont let anyone borrow them. I am afraid I might loose them but I still wear them alot anyway. <u>I think it is dangerous to wear flashy jewelry in public because there are so many thieves around and they might steal your best things but if you have something nice, you want to wear it. Its a problem.</u> My sister has a lot of jewelry. She has a collection of gold bracelets. My father and mother give her a new bracelet for a special occasion — like her first communion and when she graduated from school. She's very careful with her things. In fact, she hardly touches her bracelets herself. She keeps them locked up. I don't understand that, that's going to far. What's the point?

Deidre decided to do another freewriting, so she began by writing her kernel sentence on her paper. She freewrote for 10 minutes with this new beginning. As you can see, her second freewriting is more focused and directed than her first freewriting because she is beginning to discover what is interesting and important for her in this topic.

<u>I think it is dangerous to wear flashy jewelry in public because there are so many thieves around and they might steal your best things but if you have something nice, you want to wear it. Its a problem.</u> It's a question of rights when you think about it. Why should a thief, a criminal, have more rights than a law-abiding citizen? What I mean is, why should I not be able to wear my favorite jewelry, my gold earrings, on the train especialy at night just because a thief might steal them? That means the thief is telling me what to do, dictating my life. I don't think thats fair. On the other hand, I don't want to loose my best earrings. I feel like I'm pulled in two directions and it just makes me mad that a criminal should have that much control over a law-abiding citizen. I feel like crime is growing every day and we are giving in to it. We are adjusting to it. Like me. What I am saying is, "OK, I wont wear my best earrings." I'm going along, giving in to the criminal — letting him (or her but probably him) tell me what to do. We ought to fight back, get together and organize, not let the criminals push us around. We should organize, work together and take control over our lives.

Deidre ended up writing a research paper on private citizens' organizations to fight crime, a subject she hadn't thought much about before she did her two freewritings. As you can see, the freewriting helped her focus her ideas on an area of interest to her.

Finally, brainstorming and freewriting are techniques that help you get started. And, remember, getting started is the tough part. Once you have started, the writing process becomes much easier because you have some ideas to work with.

4.3
Choosing a Topic for Library Research

We suggest that you choose a topic related to a unit theme if you want to do a library research project. This will allow you to use some of the ideas, information, and vocabulary from the unit and thus build on knowledge you already have. Here are some suggestions for topics. However, you should feel free to suggest your own topic related to the unit theme.

Unit 1: Fashion and Style

Jewelry

Hairstyles in the 1990s

The fashion industry in _____ (a country)

Youth fashions in _____ (a country)

New fashions and styles in _____ (the current year)

_____ (your suggestion)

Unit 2: Disaster Strikes

A recent earthquake (typhoon, cyclone, hurricane, flood) in _____ (a country)

The worst earthquake (typhoon, cyclone, hurricane, flood) in _____ (a country)

Causes of earthquakes

_____ (your suggestion)

Unit 3: Across Many Cultures

Dating customs in _____ (a country)

Marriage in _____ (a country)

Divorce in _____ (a country)

Changes in _____ (a custom in some country in recent years)

_____ (your suggestion)

Unit 4: Technology: Some Interesting Effects on Our Lives

Educational television

Computers and society

How media affected a coup or revolution in _____ (a country) in _____ (a year)

How people are influenced by _____ (some kind of technology)

_____ (your suggestion)

Unit 5: How to Improve Your Memory

Description and application of another memory technique

How to remember where you put an object

Memory and age

Techniques for better studying

_____ (your suggestion)

4.4
Exploring the Topic

Go back to the "Getting Started" section, **4.2.** Start off by brainstorming about your topic and then follow up by freewriting to get ideas for your writing project. Freewrite a couple of times, if possible, to bring your ideas into focus.

When you have finished your freewriting, be sure to pick out the most interesting part or parts. Underline these parts to use later. If possible, do a second freewrite to bring your ideas into focus more clearly. Start off with your kernel.

4.5
Narrowing the Topic

Now, think of some specific questions that you want to ask about your topic.

Example: Earthquakes

1. Can people predict earthquakes in advance?
2. If so, how?
3. What is the worst earthquake in recent years? Where did it happen? How many people were killed? How much property was destroyed?
4. What causes earthquakes?

Example: Marriage Customs

1. Are marriage customs changing in _____ (a country)?
2. If so, how are they changing? Are people getting married at an older (or younger) age? Are people living together and not bothering to get married?
3. What are some of the reasons for these changes?
4. What about divorce? Is it increasing? If so, why?
5. What do people expect from marriage in today's world? Are these expectations different from those in the past? If so, how? Why?

You should try to think of at least six or seven questions, more if possible. These questions will help you focus your ideas and provide a direction for your research.

As you start doing your research, you may not be able to find information on some of your questions so it is a good idea to have several other question areas to investigate.

4.6
Developing the Topic

Look at your questions in **4.5** above. Which of your questions seem most interesting to you? Which most important?

1. Pick out three or four of your best questions. *Note:* You can change your questions at any time if you want — add new ones, combine old ones, restate them in a different way, etc. For example, you may suddenly realize that you have left a very important question out. Just add it to your list at any time.
2. Now, think about where you could get information to answer each question.

Example: Marriage Customs

Are marriage customs changing in _____ (a country)?

Sources of information: Here are some of the places you could find information to answer this question.

◆ Library (books, magazines, newspapers)
◆ Personal observation and experience
◆ Interviews

4.7
Doing Library Research

You will probably need to look up information in a library. First of all, if you have never done research in a library before, ask one of the librarians to help you. Ask the librarian where you can find information on your topic. Here are some of the library resources the librarian may suggest.

1. The card catalog

This is the place to look up books on your subject. If you look up your general subject area — for example, *marriage customs* — you can see if there are books on your subject. *Note:* You may need to think of related words and look in several places in the card catalog to find your subject (example: *marriage, living arrangements, divorce, dating customs, weddings*).

Here are examples of cards from a card catalog. Cards are filed alphabetically according to author, title of book, and general subject area. The first card is filed according to subject (in this case, *marriage*).

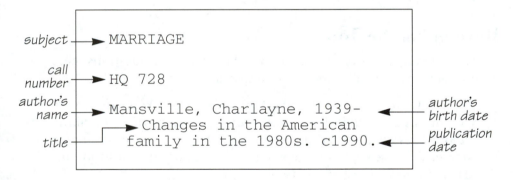

This card is filed according to author. If you knew the name of a particular author, you could look up books by that author by looking through the card catalog for the author's last name.

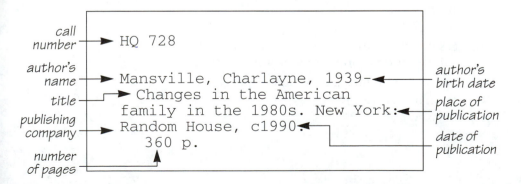

This card if filed according to title.

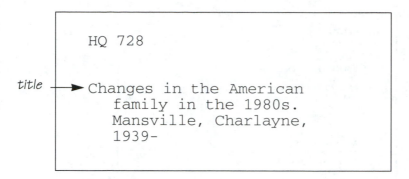

```
         HQ 728

title ───►Changes in the American
           family in the 1980s.
           Mansville, Charlayne,
           1939-
```

The *call number* tells you where to find the book in the library. Most libraries have a chart posted showing the location of books by call number areas. However, you can always ask the librarian to tell you where to find a book.

Note: In many libraries, card catalogs have now been put on computer. You can look things up in exactly the same way in a computerized catalog — alphabetically by author, book title, or general subject area. Ask a librarian to show you how to use the computer.

2. Encyclopedias

For certain types of subjects, you may be able to find general, background information in an encyclopedia. For example, if you wanted a general, historical overview of dating and marriage customs, you might look up *dating customs* and *marriage customs* in an encyclopedia. There are many specialized encyclopedias: art, music, sports, etc. You can usually get more detailed information in these specialized encyclopedias. *Note:* Encyclopedias provide a good starting point for research — but don't stop there. You need to get more specific information from other sources. Many encyclopedias include a bibliography (a list of related books) at the end of an article.

3. Readers' Guide to Periodical Literature

You can look up magazine articles on your subject here. *RGPL* is an alphabetical index by author and subject of periodicals (magazines) of general interest published in the United States, and it is arranged by year. For example, if you wanted to see what articles appeared in U.S. magazines in 1990 relating to *marriage*, you would look in the 1990 volume under "marriage."

Here is a partial listing of what you would find.

MARRIAGE
    See also
    Adultery
    Childlessness
    Common law marriage
    Divorce
    Engagement (Marriage)
    Family
    Farm marriage
    Honeymoon
    Husbands
    Interfaith marriage
    Marriage of priests
    Married couples
    Married women
    Monogamy
    Polygamy
    Remarriage
    Separation (Law)
    Weddings
    Wife abuse
    Wives

Can this marriage be saved? See issues of Ladies' Home Journal

Can we talk? [cover story; with editorial comment by Joel Guerin] M. Blau. il *American Health* 9:36-45, 96 D '90

Can you change your spouse? E. Kiester and S.V. Kiester. *Reader's Digest* 137:39-42+ S '90

Clear-thinking couples [views of Aaron Beck] S. McKee. il *American Health* 9:99 My '90

The costly retreat from marriage. B.J. Christensen. il *The Saturday Evening Post* 262:32+ Ja/F '90

Could you be a better friend to your husband? C. Johnson. il *Redbook* 175:166-7+ S '90

An excerpt from Love and other infectious diseases [illness of A. Sarris] M. Haskell. il pors *American Health* 9:66-8+ My '90

For longer life, take a wife. J. Seligmann. il *Newsweek* 116:73 N 5 '90

"Help! I married a big baby!". E. Latici. il *Redbook* 176:44-6 D '90

Holy matrimony! J. Ralston. il *Mademoiselle* 96:176-7+ Mr '90

How does your marriage grow? N. Rubin. il *Parents* 65:83-6 Ap '90

How to stay sweethearts. D. Jackson. il *Redbook* 176:94-5+ N '90

How to stop playing the blame game. G. Kessler. il *Redbook* 175:98-9 Ag '90

Ingredients of a happy marriage. A. Stoddard. *McCall's* 117:140 Je '90

Keep your marriage strong: the 8-minute love-building exercise for couples. J.B. Dilley. *Redbook* 174:84-5+ Ja '90

Keys to a loving, lasting, marriage. A.L. McGinnis. *Reader's Digest* 137:159-60+ Ag '90

Long time love. il *Essence* 21:139-40+ My '90

Love and marriage [questions and answers] C. Deutsch. See issues of *Parents* through December 1990

Making marriage work in the '90s. A. Poinsett. il *Ebony* 45:62+ Je '90

Making marriage work in the 1990s [views of Wallace Denton] il *USA Today (Periodical)* 119:4–5 N '90

Marriage & humor—a perfect union. J. Viorst. il *Redbook* 175:72+ S '90

Marriage in midlife. P. Cooper. il por *New Choices for the Best Years* 30:92 Mr '90

The next step is to write down the articles that seem to be related to your subject. Be sure to write the name of the magazine and its date of publication:

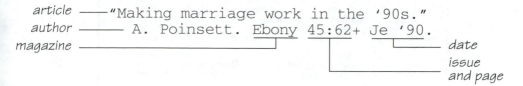

Look at the other subject categories suggested under "See also." You may find additional information in another subject category.

> **MARRIAGE**
> *See also*
> Adultery
> Childlessness
> Common law marriage
> Divorce
> Engagement (Marriage)
> Family
> Farm marriage
> Honeymoon
> Husbands
> Interfaith marriage
> Marriage of priests
> Married couples
> Married women
> Monogamy

Ask the librarian if the magazines you want are available in your library and, if so, how you may get the ones you need. Remember: *The Readers' Guide to Periodical Literature* is a good place to look for current information on your topic.

Note: If you are doing research outside of the United States, ask the librarian if the library has some sort of guide to periodical literature.

4. The New York Times Index

This is a good place to look for newspaper articles on your topic. *Note:* If your library does not have this particular index, ask the librarian if they have another index of newspaper articles. Many major newspapers have such an index.

This is a sample partial entry under the category "marriage" of articles that appeared in the *New York Times* in the year 1990. (Some of these articles might be relevant if you were researching the subject, "changes in marriage customs.")

MARRIAGES. See also
Roman Catholic Church, Je 16
   Weddings and Engagements
   Princeton University study of death rates in 16 industrial nations concludes
married people outlive unmarried people; finds unmarried men have significantly
higher death rates than married men; divorced people, especially men, have highest
death rates (Science Watch) (S), My 15,C,4:1
   Old, sacred rituals are being restored in various villages in northern Zambia, in
hopes of stemming spread of AIDS by discouraging promiscuity; Mbusa, traditional
marriage initiation ceremony among the Bemba people, noted; photo; map (M), My
30,A,4:3
   Debate is set off in Methodist church over issue of homosexual marriage, after
Bishop Joseph H. Yeakel, head of Washington Area Methodist Region, cancels
lesbian ceremony that had been approved by minister of Dumbarton Methodist
Church in Georgetown (S), Je 2,I,13:1
   Our Towns column on drama in family of Garrit and Lelia Lydecker of Riverhead,
LI, who were flabbergasted and appalled when their 16-year-old daughter Rachel,
who was in 10th grade, announced that she was in love and was going to marry an
older boy, Rich Quick, whom she had dated for a month (M), Je 22,B,1:1
   **Reform Judaism, voting for the first time to admit acknowledged, sexually
active homosexuals into its rabbinate, stops short of giving equal validity to
homosexual unions and heterosexual marriages;** action is taken at 101st annual
meeting of Central Conference of American Rabbis, Seattle (S), Je 26,A,1:5
   Rachel Quick, who married her husband, Rick, in Dec 1988, when she was 17
years old and he 19, are defying odds against so young a marriage and have won over
her parents, Garrit and Lelia Lydecker, who did not attend the wedding; photo (M) Je
26,B,1:1

Again, ask the librarian where the articles you wish to read are located.

4.8
Taking Notes

As you look through encyclopedias, newspapers, books, and other sources, you will need to take notes. In every case, you will want to:

♦ keep related information together. You should develop a way to keep your notes on each subject separate from notes on all other subjects.

♦ be able to organize and reorganize your information in different ways easily. Your notes, when they are all put together, should function as a very rough draft of your report.

There are several ways of taking notes. Two common ways are:

♦ *For a short report or composition (two or three pages)*

On separate pieces of paper, write topic headings, one topic per page (example: causes of earthquakes, ways of predicting earthquakes, damage caused by some recent major earthquakes).

As you find information relating to a topic, make notes on the page that deals with that topic. Do not mix topics on one page. If you find that a topic becomes longer or more complex than you expected, divide it onto separate pages, one page for each new subtopic. For each note that you write down, remember to include the source where you got the information (the book/magazine title, author, date of publication, page number).

When you are finished taking notes, number the points on each page in the order in which you want to use them in your report. You can then organize these pages into the general format of your report. The information on sources will be useful for quotations, footnotes, and references.

♦ *For longer reports and general note taking:*
The most common way to take notes is on 3 by 5 inch index cards. Generally, you use one card per item of information. At the top of each card, write the topic and the source, then use the card to write out the information you want. (Rather than repeating the full information about the source on each card, you may want to keep a separate list with this information — title, author, date of publication — and just write the title and page number on each index card.)

When you are finished with your research, you may have up to several hundred cards for a long report. You can then organize and reorganize these cards into the format for your report.

You may be interested to learn that the glossary in this text was developed on index cards, one word per card. Several possible definitions and example sentences were written on each card. The authors then looked over all the cards and selected the definitions and examples they wished to use. Cards for cross-referenced words were added, and all the cards were alphabetized. It was then easy to type the final version.

4.9
Quoting and Paraphrasing

When you are using information from books and articles, it is important to know how to quote and how to paraphrase.

1. Quoting

When you are using the *exact words* from a book or article, you must use quotation marks around these words to show that you are borrowing someone else's words.

Example:
"What's new in fashion this season is denim, denim, denim. And not just for blue jeans. In fact, it's for everything BUT blue jeans — coats, dresses, suits. In past years, denim was sporty and casual. This year, 1991, it's classy and it can go anywhere."

Note: The quotation marks (") go at the beginning of the quoted passage and at the end of the quoted passage("......"). The final quotation mark goes after the period or the question mark.

In Milan, Italy, designer Franco Moschino says, "I use denim as a symbol of our times. It fits in everywhere. And, very important, it makes everyone look young — or younger."

Directly quoting (using the exact words of someone else) can be quite effective if
- ◆ the information is very important
- ◆ the ideas are well-expressed
- ◆ the statement is made by an important person; for example, a recognized expert in the field or a highly-placed official.

Example:
"The United States has one of the shortest school years of any industrialized country in the world, and American students are falling behind. It's time for a change," says Ernest L. Boyer, president of the Carnegie Foundation for the Advancement of Teaching. ⎤— *expert*

On the other hand, *do not quote*:
- ◆ *too much.* A very long quote (a page or more) is not effective. Just pick out the most important information to quote.
- ◆ *everyday, commonplace information.*
  "The weather in Belgium is often rainy. However, there were several sunny days in July."
  This information is not important enough to directly quote.
- ◆ *too often.* Quotes become ineffective and meaningless if you have too many of them. Save quotes for something special.

2. Paraphrasing
When you restate an idea in your own words, you are paraphrasing. Notice the difference between quoting and paraphrasing in the following example:

Quoting: Ernest Boyer, president of the Carnegie Foundation for the Advancement of Teaching, says, "The time has come to increase the length of the American school year. The U.S. ranks tenth among industrialized nations in the length of the school year. If we are to match their record of achievement, a radical change is necessary."

Paraphrasing: According to Ernest Boyer, president of the Carnegie Foundation for the Advancement of Teaching, the U.S. should increase the length of the school year to match that of other industrialized nations.

Quoting should be saved for the special situations discussed in Section 1 above. In other situations, it is preferable to paraphrase — to restate an idea in your own words.

Here is another example of the difference between quoting and paraphrasing. You decide which is a quote and which is a paraphrase.

Ruth Sidel states that women and their children comprise most of the poor people in the United States today.

According to Ruth Sidel, "Of poor people in the United States today, the vast majority are women and their children."

4.10
Footnotes and Bibliography

You show the sources for your information in the footnotes and the bibliography.

1. Footnotes

Your reader often wants to know where you got your information or you may need to prove where your information came from, particularly if you are dealing with an unusual or surprising bit of information. You should always footnote important information and direct quotes. There are several ways to footnote. After the statement to be footnoted in your report, you write a number. The first footnote would be "1," the second one "2," etc. The number should be written above the line.

Example:
The gross national product fell by .4 percent between July and September.[1]

At the bottom of the page — or at the end of the paper on a special page entitled *Footnotes* — you cite the reference from which you got this information. In other words, you tell your reader where you got your information. Ask your teacher where you should put your footnotes (at the bottom of the page or at the end of the paper) and the footnote form you should use. Your teacher may refer you to a style sheet such as the *MLA [Modern Language Association] Style Sheet*, which will explain and illustrate how to write footnotes.

Here are some sample footnotes.

Book

[1] Thomas S. Szasz, *Ideology and Insanity: Essays on the Psychiatric Dehumanization of Man* (Garden City, NY: Doubleday Anchor, 1990), pp. 113–139.

Article

[2] Robert Pear, "Who Really Needs to Be at St. Elizabeths?" *Washington Star*, August 9, 1991, p. A–1.

Footnotes are sometimes used to give additional information about a point mentioned in the report. Here is an example.

Additional Information

[3] For more information on this subject, see John Thompson, *The First Cities* (London, 1983), pp. 18–71.

2. Bibliography

A bibliography is a complete list of all sources of information you have used in the report: books, articles, interviews. The bibliography (sometimes called *References*) goes at the end of your paper. At the top of the page, you should write the word BIBLIOGRAPHY (or REFERENCES). Then you should list all of your sources alphabetically by the author's last name.

Ask your teacher what bibliographic form you should use. Here is a sample of a partial bibliography.

Bibliography

Dickens, Mary Ellen, and Margaret Haddad. "New Models of Reading Instruction." *The Reading Journal,* 19:26-29. March, 1989.

Gardiner, John. *Patterns of Immigration in the 1980s.* New York: Harper & Row Publishers, 1988.

Gonzales, David. Personal Interview. London, May 12, 1989.

4.11
Interviewing

In addition to doing library research on your topic, you can get information about your topic by interviewing people. Here are some important points to keep in mind when you are setting up and conducting an interview.

1. Deciding on interview information areas

Think about what kind of information you want to get in an interview. Let us suppose that your topic is "single parent families." You could interview some single parents to get information about their experiences as single parents.

If your topic were "divorce," you could interview someone who had had direct experience with divorce, for example, someone who had been divorced or whose parents had been divorced.

2. Making up interview questions

After you have decided upon what kind of information you want to get in an interview (Section 1 above), you should make up a general list of interview questions. Try to think of questions that might elicit interesting answers that are related to your topic.

You should have some yes-no questions —

Example:
Were you very much affected by your parents' divorce?

AND some open-ended information gathering questions
(Why...? What do you think about...? How would you...? etc.)

Example:
What are some of the most difficult aspects of divorce from your experience?

Show your list of questions to two or three other people, if possible, and ask for their suggestions.

3. Selecting people to interview

Now you should choose some people to interview. Generally, two or three interviews are enough unless you are doing a long, in-depth study. Then you will need more. Ideally, the people you interview should have

- ◆ some direct experience related to the topic (e.g., some type of experience with divorce if you were researching divorce)

OR

- ◆ some important information or knowledge related to the topic. In other words, the person could be an expert in the area or an official who would have access to such information.

4. Conducting the interview

Always try to arrange your interviews at a time of convenience to the interviewee. You will get better results if you do. Try to be as relaxed and cordial as possible when you conduct your interviews to make your interviewees feel at ease. Listen carefully and be sure to ask additional questions if something interesting but unexpected comes up. Make brief notes to help you remember important responses. Jot down just enough information to help you reconstruct the essential information later, but don't try to write down everything.

Example:
What are some of the problems you have faced as a result of being divorced?

loneliness, isolation, not enough money

Be sure to thank your interviewee for taking the time for the interview and ask if you may check back with him or her later for additional information. You may find that you would like to ask another question or two later as you are looking over your notes.

Try to write up your interviews in some form as quickly as possible so that you don't forget essential information.

5. Using interview information

When you are writing your paper, in the body of the paper you can include information from your interviews.

♦ *Explain who you interviewed*

Denise Arroyo is a divorced mother with two small children in Los Angeles. In a recent interview, Ms. Arroyo stated that . . . .[1]

You should footnote this information so that your reader will know when the interview was conducted.

♦ *Quote sparingly and paraphrase extensively*

Write up most of the interview in third-person, narrative form. In other words, paraphrase most of the interview. If your interviewee made a statement that was particularly important or well-expressed, then directly quote that statement. But, remember, don't quote too much! (You may wish to review the guidelines for quoting and paraphrasing in Sections 1 and 2 on page 175).

5.1
Making an Outline

After you have gathered information from a variety of sources, you can then begin to write your paper. Some people find it useful to make a general outline of how they want to organize their paper. Here is an example of an outline.

Effects of the 1985 Earthquake in Mexico City

I. Introduction — General overview of the subject
   A. What happened
   B. When it happened
   C. Where: Mexico City
   D. General statement about damage and effects

II. Body
   A. Description of the earthquake
      1. How strong it was and how long it lasted
      2. Time of day it occurred — what people were doing at that time
      3. Aftershocks — how many, how strong, effects
   B. How people were affected
      1. Statistics on deaths and injuries
      2. People who were most affected — why (specific case studies, if possible)
   C. Damage to property
      1. Description of property damage
         a. statistics about damage
         b. location of property
      2. Examples of different types of property damage
         a. older buildings
         b. newer skyscrapers
         c. hospitals — explanation of consequences
   D. Rescue and relief efforts
      1. National and international involvement
         a. statistics on money relief
         b. involvement of people and description of efforts
            1. examples of heroic efforts
      2. Problems in rescue efforts
         a. collapse of hospitals, etc.
         b. lack of medical and other supplies
         c. transportation/sanitation problems
   E. Lessons to be learned from this earthquake
      1. Importance of earthquake-proof building construction
      2. Importance of being ready for disaster emergencies
      3. Having sufficient medical, food, water sources and supplies
      4. People being trained to respond to disaster emergencies

III. Conclusion
   A. Summary
   B. Suggestions and recommendations for the future

Note: Many people find it useful to make a general outline before they begin writing. They believe the process of making an outline helps them plan and organize their ideas. When they are writing their paper or report, they can refer to their outline to make sure that they have not forgotten any parts. On the other hand, other people believe that they can organize and express their ideas more clearly if they do NOT make an outline before they begin.

Make an outline of your topic now, but DON'T be afraid to change it as necessary once you begin actually writing. DON'T be locked in by your outline. Use the outline as a way of thinking about the organization and content of your report and as a guide.

5.2
The Parts of a Composition

Most compositions and reports have four main parts, and each part has a specific function.

+ **Title:** This is the name of your report or composition, and it should give the reader some idea of what the report or composition will cover.

    Example:

    THE AMERICAN SCHOOL YEAR: TIME FOR A CHANGE?

+ **Introduction:** Here is where you give the background of your subject and a general overview of what the paper or report will be about. It should give the reader a basic idea of what you will cover in general terms. Your thesis (main idea of the composition) should be clearly stated in the introduction.

    Example of a thesis statement:
    The American school year must be extended if American students are going to keep up with students from other industrialized countries.

+ **Body:** Here is where you give reasons and examples to support your thesis statement. Generally, you state a reason, explain it if necessary, and then give specific examples to illustrate this reason. It is a good idea to put in as many facts and relevant figures as possible here.

    Examples of body paragraphs:
    The American 180-day school year is based on a rural tradition that no longer fits the needs of a heavily-industrialized, urban society. In the past, most American families

lived on farms, and they needed their children to help them with the farm work in the summers, especially during harvest. Consequently, the school year was designed to give students a three-month vacation in the summer so they could work on the family farm. However, less than three percent of Americans live on farms now, so there is no longer a need for such a long summer vacation to supply farm labor.

Ernest L. Boyer, president of the Carnegie Foundation for the Advancement of Teaching, says, "The time has come for radical change in the American school year if American students are to keep pace with students from the top industrial countries around the world."[2] Boyer proposes a longer school year so that American students can cover more material, particularly in math and science.

Note: If a quote is five lines or shorter, it does not have to be indented and presented as a separate paragraph (see Boyer quote above). It simply continues as part of the text and quotation marks are used around the quote. If the quote is longer than five lines, however, it should be indented and presented as a separate paragraph. Quotation marks should NOT be used.

Example of a longer quote:
Ernest L. Boyer, president of the Carnegie Foundation for the Advancement of Teaching, says,

> *The time has come for radical change in the American school year if American students are to keep pace with students from the top industrial countries around the world. Japanese students go to school 243 days a year, while American students go just 180 days. American students simply cannot keep up.[3]*

The body is the longest part of a composition. It contains the specific information, concrete examples, and statistics (see paragraph above). The length of the body varies according to the length of your report or composition. In a short composition, the body might be two or three paragraphs. In a long report, the body would be many pages.

- ◆ *Conclusion*: You restate the thesis in slightly different words, briefly review the major points of your report, and make a few general remarks about the thesis. Do NOT introduce any new information here. You may want to compare, contrast, or highlight some information that you thought was especially important in the body. Also, people frequently make recommendations for some sort of change in the conclusion based upon the findings in their report.

Remember: The conclusion is a kind of brief summary; keep it short. If the reader has not read the whole report or composition, the reader should be able to read the conclusion and get a general idea of the whole report or composition.

Example:
In conclusion, educational experts agree that it is time to extend the American school year. The 180-day year, with its long summer vacation, no longer fits the needs of our urban, industrial society, and we cannot keep up with other industrialized countries where students go to school up to 63 days more a year. As Ernest Boyer says, "It's time for a change, a radical change."

5.3
Writing and Getting Feedback on the First Draft

In this section, we give you suggestions for how to write the first draft of your report and get feedback on it.

1. Writing the first draft

Beginning with any part of your report, write the first draft. *Note:* You do not have to write the introduction first. If you find it easier to begin with the body, start there. You may wish to write in pencil and double or triple-space so that you have room to make changes as you go along. As you are writing, read over what you have just written from time to time. This can help you get ideas for continuing.

2. Getting feedback on the first draft

Show your draft to at least one other person. Ask them to tell you what parts they like best and what parts are unclear or incomplete and need to be changed. Where do you need to have more information? More examples? Which points are unclear? Be sure to discuss problem areas thoroughly so that you can decide how to rewrite them. Concentrate primarily on ideas and making sure they are expressed clearly. Don't worry about form (grammar, punctuation, and spelling) yet. That will come later.

5.4
Writing and Getting Feedback on the Second Draft

In this section, we give you some suggestions on how to use feedback on your first draft to revise and then how to edit your report for form.

1. Using feedback to revise content

After you have discussed the changes suggested to you by the person giving you feedback on your first draft, you should write your composition again trying to incorporate these changes. Usually this means that you have to add examples and perhaps explain how these examples are connected to your main points. Maybe your introduction was not as strong as it could have been. Whatever the problem areas are, now is the time to clear them up. At this point, your goals are to make your ideas as clear and as complete as possible. You should be trying to establish a closer connection with your reader and making it as easy as possible for your reader to understand your meaning.

As you are writing your second draft, read it over to yourself to see if you are making your ideas clear.

2. Getting feedback on the second draft

Show your second draft to the person or persons who read your first draft. Make sure your revisions are clear. If your ideas are still not clear or complete, write in the necessary changes.

3. Editing for form

When the meaning is clear, check over grammar, punctuation, and spelling with the person or persons reading your draft. *Note:* Don't worry about grammar, punctuation, and spelling until the meaning is clear.

Try to learn to recognize your problem areas in form. For example, do you sometimes make mistakes in verb endings, e.g., leaving off **-s** or **-ed**? Do you mix up "there," "their," and "they're" sometimes? Or "its" and "it's"? Try to identify and correct these errors in form at this time.

5.5
Writing the Final Draft

Write or type your final draft. If you write your final draft by hand, be sure to use a pen. Write neatly and clearly on lined paper. It is usually advisable to skip lines because it will be easier for your reader to read. If you type, double-space. Hand in your final draft to your teacher.

If you write several drafts of a paper, the final product will be much better. Also, remember to concentrate on content (clear expression of ideas) first, and then work on form (grammar, punctuation, and spelling).

One final note: GOOD WRITING IS REWRITING. All good writers are really rewriters.

GLOSSARY

In this glossary, words are defined as they are used in the readings. Since many of these words may also have other meanings, you may want to look in your own dictionary for the full range of meanings of a word. Page numbers refer to the page on which a word appears in this book.

achieve *v.* To accomplish; to succeed. *Ex.* Mrs. Sidki achieved her goal of becoming a dentist. (p. 98)

activate *v.* To start up; to set in motion. *Ex.* If a fire starts, the smoke will activate the smoke alarm and wake you up.

admire *v.* To praise; to take an interest in. *Ex.* I admire your ability to ice-skate so well. (p. 74)

affect *v.* To influence. *Ex.* Does television advertising affect what you buy? (p. 93)

against all odds *phrase.* Something happening although it seems impossible. *Ex.* Against all odds, Alfonso learned to walk again after the accident. (p. 114)

ajangle *adj.* (an unusual form of *jangling*). Overexcited; vibrating. *Ex.* My head was ajangle when everyone tried to talk to me at the same time. (p. 116)

alert *v.* To warn. *Ex.* We will alert you if anything unusual happens. (p. 106)

alter *v.* To change. *Ex.* Please don't alter your plans just for me. (p. 14)

amid *prep.* In the middle of. *Ex.* Some beautiful flowers grew amid the grass and weeds in the field.

anxiety *n.* Worry; concern. *Ex.* Did you feel much anxiety during the earthquake? (p. 84)

anxiously *adv.* In a worried manner. *Ex.* The students waited anxiously to see their test scores. (p. 45)

apologize *v.* To say you are sorry. *Ex.* I apologize for being late. (p. 127)

apparently *adv.* Having the appearance of. *Ex.* Mr. Calvin looks tired; apparently, he didn't sleep well last night. (p. 85)

application *n.* A way to use something. *Ex.* Word processing and accounting are two applications of computer technology. (p. 93)

appreciate *v.* To be grateful or thankful. *Ex.* I appreciate your help very much. (p. 97)

aristocrat *n.* Connected to royalty; from a high social class. *Ex.* The king surrounded himself with aristocrats. (p. 16)

aroma *n.* A strong, pleasant smell. *Ex.* I love the aroma of fresh baked bread.

as yet *phrase.* Up to now. *Ex.* As yet, we haven't heard anything about their plans. (p. 83)

ascertain *v.* To get information; to find out. *Ex.* First you must ascertain how far it is to Miami, and then you can decide how long it will take to get there. (p. 116)

assemble *v.* To gather together. *Ex.* The committee will assemble at 7:30 P.M. and finish at 9 P.M. (p. 82)

associate *v.* To connect; to join together. *Ex.* I associate champagne with France and vodka with Russia. (p. 129)

assured *adj.* guaranteed; certain; positive. *Ex.* I was assured by my teacher that I had passed the test. (p. 86)

attempt *v.* To try. *Ex.* The magician said, "I will attempt to make this rabbit disappear." (p. 74)

attribute *v.* To think something is caused by a particular fact. *Ex.* Experts attribute much air pollution to cars, buses, and trucks. (p. 115)

auspicious *adj.* favorable; good luck. *Ex.* In many Asian countries, people plan weddings on auspicious days. (p. 85)

automatically *adv.* Happening by itself or without assistance. *Ex.* I automatically wake up at 6:30 every morning; I don't need an alarm clock. (p. 99)

awe *n.* A feeling of amazement and respect. *Ex.* They stared in awe at the Grand Canyon. (p. 118)

bare *adj.* Empty; not covered. *Ex.* The room was completely bare, without even one chair in it. (p. 96)

be deprived of *v.* To have something taken away. *Ex.* The thief was deprived of his freedom during his two years in jail. (p. 65)

beeper *n.* A device that makes short, repeated sounds to attract your attention. *Ex.* Doctors often carry beepers so they can be reached in an emergency. (p. 106)

bidding (do one's bidding) *v.* To do what one is told; to follow an order. *Ex.* Children are taught to do their parents' bidding. (p. 115)

blast out *v.* To play very loudly. *Ex.* The car drove around the city blasting out messages for the political candidate over a loudspeaker. (p. 98)

bleach *v.* To remove or lighten the color. *Ex.* If you bleach your hair from brown to blond, no one will recognize you! (p. 2)

bolt *v.* To run or jump up suddenly. *Ex.* The cat bolted up the tree. (p. 116)

brief *adj.* Very short. *Ex.* Give me a brief description of the book. (p. 53)

brilliant *adj.* Very intelligent; clever. *Ex.* Shakespeare was a brilliant writer of plays. (p. 86)

brilliantly *adv.* Full of light; very bright. *Ex.* The sun shone brilliantly all day. (p. 87)

bulletin *n.* An announcement of new information. *Ex.* Did you receive the bulletin describing the class schedule for next semester? (p. 98)

bumpy *adj.* Uneven; with sudden movements. *Ex.* The airplane ride was bumpy during the storm. (p. 82)

by hook or by crook *phrase.* Somehow; one way or another. *Ex.* By hook or by crook, I'm going to finish college even if it takes me 10 years. (p. 114)

by their own devices *phrase.* Creating and using their own plan. *Ex.* Orienteering is a sport where people go out into the woods until they are lost, and then they get back by their own devices using only a map and compass. (p. 149)

catchy *adj.* Easily remembered. *Ex.* Everyone is whistling that catchy song.

celebration *n.* A joyful occasion. *Ex.* Please come to the celebration of my parents' 40th wedding anniversary. (p. 53)

century *n.* A period of 100 years. *Ex.* The year 2000 is the beginning of the 21st century. (p. 93)

ceremonial *adj.* Very formal and polite, sometimes involving a ritual. *Ex.* Will you attend only the ceremonial part of the wedding or come to the party too? (p. 96)

chance *n.* Probability; possibility. *Ex.* What are the chances of winning the lottery? (p. 35)

clarity *n.* The ability to think clearly. *Ex.* Ambroise explained the problem with such clarity that everyone understood it. (p. 117)

clue *n.* Information that helps you solve a problem. *Ex.* Do the police have any clues about the person who stole the money? (p. 43)

coincide *v.* To happen at the same time. *Ex.* Since my birthday coincides with Independence Day, my birthday is always a holiday! (p. 85)

collapse *v.* To fall down suddenly. *Ex.* If the stock market collapses, Mr. Johnson will lose all his money. (p. 32)

compile *v.* To collect and put together; to gather. *Ex.* Serya compiled a list of all the countries she would like to visit. (p. 96)

complex *adj.* Complicated; hard to understand. *Ex.* The instructions for using this computer are very complex. (p. 35)

compliment *n.* A statement of praise or admiration. *Ex.* She received many compliments for her excellent work. (p. 129)

component *n.* A part of something. *Ex.* I think that good health, good friends, and a good job are the components of a happy life. (p. 125)

composure *n.* The ability to stay calm; controlling your emotions. *Ex.* Marina lost her composure and got angry when the waiter dropped the food in her lap. (p. 116)

compulsive *adj.* Uncontrollable; feeling that you must do something. *Ex.* I have a compulsive desire to keep my house very neat and clean. (p. 104)

concentration *n.* Paying attention carefully; thinking very hard. *Ex.* I'm trying to study but the noise outside is disturbing my concentration. (p. 127)

concrete *adj.* Specific; definite. *Ex.* He spoke in a general way and didn't give any concrete suggestions. (p. 86)

condemn *v.* To be punished; to suffer. *Ex.* The prisoner was condemned to 30 years in jail. (p. 119)

confirm *v.* To make sure something is correct; to verify. *Ex.* Three days before a flight, you should confirm your airplane reservation. (p. 86)

confiscate *v.* To take something away because it is forbidden. *Ex.* If you try to bring fruit into the United States from abroad, customs agents will confiscate it from you at the border. (p. 98)

confront *v.* To come face to face; to challenge. *Ex.* She confronted me with the evidence and I agreed she was correct. (p. 117)

consequence *n.* A result that happens naturally; a necessary result. *Ex.* As a consequence of quitting my job, I had to use my savings to pay my rent. (p. 46)

conservative *adj.* Moderate; not taking chances. *Ex.* My conservative estimate is that it will take at least 12-14 days to finish the project. (p. 46)

conservatively *adv.* Modestly; in a way that avoids attention. *Ex.* If you don't know the local customs, it is best to act conservatively. (p. 74)

considerable *adj.* A large amount. *Ex.* She earns a considerable amount of money as a lawyer. (p. 86)

contend *v.* To believe; to state an opinion. *Ex.* Some researchers contend that Vitamin C helps prevent colds.

control subjects *n.* The people who do not receive the treatment in a scientific experiment so they can be compared to the group that does receive the treatment. *Ex.* In the cholesterol test, one group ate a low-fat diet for eight weeks; the control subjects were allowed to eat anything they wanted. (p. 149)

conventional *adj.* Usual; standard. *Ex.* It is conventional for cars to have four wheels, but some mini-cars have three wheels. (p. 99)

corpse *n.* A dead body. *Ex.* Mystery stories often begin with the discovery of a corpse. (p. 146)

costume *n.* Traditional or unusual clothing. *Ex.* Everyone came to the party dressed in costumes of famous kings or queens. (p. 96)

crack *n.* A small opening; a break. *Ex.* If you look through the crack in the fence, you can see the beautiful garden. (p. 34)

crack down *v.* To enforce the law strictly. *Ex.* In order to crack down on speeding cars, the police gave lots of tickets. (p. 97)

crisis *n.* A very serious situation; an emergency. *Ex.* My father's death was a terrible crisis for my family. (p. 97)

critical *adj.* Important; necessary. *Ex.* It is critical that you get there on time.

crush *v.* To push something down until it is flat. *Ex.* The cook crushed some tomatoes to make the spaghetti sauce. (p. 32)

cue *n.* A reminder; a signal. *Ex.* When I give the cue, would everyone please stand up. (p. 148)

cure *n.* Treatment that takes care of an illness or problem. *Ex.* Aspirin is the usual cure for a headache. (p. 93)

customary *adj.* Usual; traditional. *Ex.* It is customary to take off your shoes before entering a Japanese home. (p. 72)

dagger *n.* A short knife used as a weapon. *Ex.* In the movies, pirates always carry daggers in their belts. (p. 148)

damage *v.* To hurt; to harm. *Ex.* The flood damaged the houses that were near the river. (p. 32)

deal with *v.* To concern; to discuss. *Ex.* This book deals with modern art. (p. 64)

decorate *v.* To make something more beautiful by adding colorful or attractive things to it. *Ex.* Japanese families decorate their houses with pine branches for the New Year's celebration. (p. 83)

deep down *phrase.* Having a very strong feeling about something; a secret desire. *Ex.* Paolo works as an accountant, but deep down in his heart he really wants to be an artist. (p. 128)

demeaning *adj.* Insulting; implying inferior status. *Ex.* In some parts of Asia, it is demeaning to show people the bottom of your feet or shoes. (p. 73)

deprived see *be deprived of.*

detect *v.* To discover. *Ex.* Can you detect the orange flavor in these cookies? (p. 45)

determine *v.* 1. To decide firmly. *Ex.* Alice is determined to finish college even if she has to go at night. (p. 53) 2. To figure out. *Ex.* John determined how many people were coming to the party, and then he went shopping for the food. (p. 44)

devastating *adj.* Causing great damage; destructive. *Ex.* The heavy rains caused devastating floods all along the river. (p. 52)

devices see *by their own devices.*

dictator *n.* A person who has complete power in a country. *Ex.* The Tran family was glad to escape from life under a dictator. (p. 98)

disaster *n.* Great harm; terrible destruction. *Ex.* Oil spills have caused terrible disasters in the ocean. (p. 52)

discretion *n.* Good judgment and caution. *Ex.* If someone else is paying for your dinner in a restaurant, use discretion when choosing from the menu. (p. 74)

discriminating *adj.* Making knowledgeable choices; recognizing good quality. *Ex.* Ferdinand has a discriminating taste in furniture; he buys beautiful antiques. (p. 107)

distant *adj.* Far away. *Ex.* The year 2075 is in the distant future. (p. 125)

distract *v.* To take your attention away from something. *Ex.* Pardon me, I got distracted by the noise outside and didn't hear what you said. (p. 106)

distressed *adj.* Worried and unhappy; anxious. *Ex.* The child was very distressed when her dog ran away. (p. 104)

diversion *n.* An activity that turns your attention from something serious to something that amuses or relaxes you. *Ex.* Movies are my favorite diversion when I want to relax. (p. 106)

do wonders *v.* To be happily surprised; to give excellent results. *Ex.* The advertisement says this cream will do wonders for dry skin. (p. 64)

droop *v.* To hang down weakly (with no strength). *Ex.* The flowers will droop if you don't give them enough water. (p. 107)

dye *v.* To change the color by washing in a colored liquid. *Ex.* I plan to dye these white curtains green to match my green carpet. (p. 2)

easy chair *n.* A large, comfortable chair. *Ex.* Every evening I sit in my favorite easy chair to read the newspaper and watch TV. (p. 148)

eavesdrop *v.* To listen secretly. *Ex.* Cynthia eavesdropped on the plans for the party, so she knew about it before anyone else. (p. 85)

eerie *adj.* Strange and mysterious; weird. *Ex.* The wind made eerie noises as it blew through the trees. (p. 136)

effect *n.* A result. *Ex.* Drinking too much coffee has a bad effect on me; I get nervous. (p. 93)

elope *v.* To go away secretly to get married, usually against the parents' wishes. *Ex.* Ruth and Gary eloped on Tuesday but didn't tell their families until Friday. (p. 116)

emerge *v.* To come out. *Ex.* The sun emerged from behind the clouds. (p. 115)

encourage *v.* To support; to give someone confidence to do something. *Ex.* The coach encouraged the swimming team to swim as fast as possible. (p. 4)

engaged *adj.* Planning to marry. *Ex.* Juan and Maria became engaged last month; they will marry next year. (p. 64)

enormous *adj.* Very large. *Ex.* Carlos ate an enormous bowl of rice for dinner because he was so hungry. (p. 34)

erupt *v.* To burst out; to break out. *Ex.* Fire erupted from the burning building. (p. 24)

eruption *n.* See *erupt.* *Ex.* The volcanic eruption destroyed the village. (p. 44)

essential *adj.* Necessary. *Ex.* It is essential that you get here by 8 A.M. (p. 114)

estimate *v.* To guess approximately. *Ex.* I estimate that it will take six hours to drive from Los Angeles to San Francisco. (p. 34)

evaluate *v.* To analyze; to compare the good and bad points. *Ex.* We evaluated all the choices and decided to buy a used car instead of a new one. (p. 34)

event *n.* Something that happens. *Ex.* What has been the most important event in your life so far? (p. 44)

evil spirit *n.* A supernatural being that causes harm or misfortune. *Ex.* Some people believe that evil spirits cause their illnesses. (p. 118)

exclusion *n.* Not being part of something; being left out. *Ex.* The exclusion of Mr. Murphy from the conversation was rude. (p. 53)

extend *v.* 1. To offer; to hold out (one's hand). *Ex.* We extend our best wishes to you and your family. (p. 72) 2. To go beyond; to go past. *Ex.* Highway 5 extends beyond San Francisco all the way to Los Angeles. (p. 107)

extremely *adv.* Very much. *Ex.* I went to bed early last night because I was extremely tired. (p. 43)

factor *n.* One part. *Ex.* I can't go on vacation because of two factors — no time and no money. (p. 35)

fad *n.* Something that is popular for a short time. *Ex.* Cowboy boots are the current fad among college students. (p. 24)

faded *adj.* Having lost color or brightness. *Ex.* I wear faded, old clothing when I wash my car. (p. 119)

fall short *v. phrase.* To fail to reach a goal. *Ex.* I tried to save enough money for a new car, but I fell short and had to buy a used one.

fare *v.* (old-fashioned word). To do. *Ex.* Harold fared well in the spelling contest, and he won second prize. (p. 106)

feat *n.* A great accomplishment. *Ex.* Did you read about the man who performed the feat of skiing down Mt. Everest? (p. 147)

figure out *v.* To understand; to solve a problem. *Ex.* I can't figure out how to work this VCR. (p. 13)

flatter *v.* To say nice things about someone so he or she will feel good. *Ex.* You flatter me with your kind words. (p. 129)

flickering *adj.* Giving off light that changes back and forth suddenly from bright to dim. *Ex.* The flickering candles and violin music made the restaurant seem very romantic. (p. 119)

flood *v.* To fill with too much water. *Ex.* The broken pipes flooded my bathroom. (p. 95)

flustered *adj.* Embarrassed and nervous. *Ex.* I get flustered every time I have to make a speech. (p. 127)

fool *v.* To trick; to make a person believe something that is not true. *Ex.* You can't fool me! A real diamond costs a lot more than that.

189

for his (her, my) sake *phrase.* For someone's benefit. *Ex.* Please do it for my sake even if you don't want to do it for yourself. (p. 84)

for openers *phrase.* Something that happens first. *Ex.* For openers, let's start dinner with some soup. (p. 64)

formula *n.* General rule; code. *Ex.* The chemical formula for water is H_2O. (p. 74)

fraction of a second *phrase.* A very short time. [A fraction is a small part of something. A second is 1/60 of a minute.] *Ex.* It takes only a fraction of a second for a calculator to add the numbers. (p. 137)

fragrant *adj.* Having a beautiful smell. *Ex.* Roses are very fragrant flowers. (p. 86)

furtive *adj.* Secret; not obvious. *Ex.* His furtive behavior made everyone nervous. (p. 83)

generosity *n.* Willingness to give help or money to others. *Ex.* The hospital was built through the generosity of many people. (p. 74)

ghostlike *adj.* Looking like a ghost. *Ex.* The people walking past me in the heavy fog seemed ghostlike. (p. 96)

give out *v.* To distribute. *Ex.* The theater gave out free tickets to the winners of the contest. (p. 45)

glance *n.* A quick look. *Ex.* He glanced out the window and saw the children playing on the sidewalk. (p. 85)

glib *adj.* Making difficult things sound easy. *Ex.* The salesman's glib remarks about how easy it would be to "buy now, pay later" made me uncomfortable. (p. 104)

glimpse *n.* A quick look; a glance. *Ex.* From the train window, you can catch quick glimpses of the countryside. (p. 83)

go forward *v.* To proceed; to go ahead. *Ex.* Unless it rains, we will go forward with our plans for a picnic tomorrow. (p. 54)

grin *v.* To have a big smile. *Ex.* Mustaffah grinned when he heard the good news. (p. 84)

harness *v.* To get control over something. *Ex.* The Aswan Dam harnessed the energy of the Nile River to make electricity. (p. 99)

heap *v.* To pile up. *Ex.* My mother heaped so much food on my plate that I couldn't finish it. (p. 83)

heartily *adv.* With great enjoyment; with enthusiasm. *Ex.* Mr. Anton greeted his guests heartily. (p. 64)

heavy-duty *adj.* Strong and long-lasting; can be used for hard work. *Ex.* The cover of this book is made of heavy-duty paper. (p. 23)

hesitate *v.* To stop for a short time while you decide what to do or say. *Ex.* Don't hesitate to call me if you need some help. (p. 96)

hold up *v.* To remain in good condition; to last. *Ex.* My health has held up well even though I've been working very hard. (p. 23)

huge *adj.* Very large. *Ex.* What would you do if you had a huge amount of money? (p. 86)

hypothesis *n.* An idea about something which is not proven. *Ex.* The astronomer had a hypothesis for why there are canals on Mars, but not everyone agreed with her. (p. 104)

hysterically *adv.* With uncontrolled emotion or excitement. *Ex.* She shouted hysterically, "Run, run, the building is collapsing!" (p. 119)

idle *adj.* Having nothing to do. *Ex.* A person who has lots of hobbies is rarely idle. (p. 107)

illumination *n.* The amount of light. *Ex.* The illumination in the library has to be very bright for reading. (p. 87)

image *n.* The way something looks; a picture. *Ex.* Mr. Cardenas is the image of his grandfather. (p. 117)

immigrant *n.* A person who leaves his native country to live in another country. *Ex.* Canada has many immigrants from Eastern Europe. (p. 23)

in common *phrase.* Shared by everyone. *Ex.* My sister and I have lots of interests in common. (p. 95)

in ruin *phrase.* Destroyed. *Ex.* All my furniture was in ruin after the fire. (p. 52)

industrialist *n.* A person who owns or runs a large manufacturing company. *Ex.* One of the most famous industrialists in the United States was Henry Ford. (p. 117)

infrequent *adj.* Seldom; not often. *Ex.* Snow is infrequent in Florida. (p. 46)

initial *adj.* First; in the beginning. *Ex.* It is important to make a good initial impression on a job interview. (p. 115)

injure *v.* To hurt; to damage. *Ex.* Two people were seriously injured in that automobile accident. (p. 32)

innocence *n.* Simplicity; without much experience in life. *Ex.* Children begin life in innocence. (p. 15)

inquire *v.* To ask a question. *Ex.* Mr. Lee inquired about the price of a new car. (p. 72)

instinct *n.* Something that happens naturally (without thinking about it). *Ex.* Plants have an instinct to turn towards the light. (p. 140)

intended *adj.* Expected; planned. *Ex.* The scientific experiment had the intended results. (p. 94)

interfere *v.* To get in the way of. *Ex.* Does the noise from the street interfere with your studying? (p. 64)

intrusion *n.* Interference; going in where you are not wanted. *Ex.* Would it be an intrusion if we came to visit you early in the morning? (p. 72)

invaluable *adj.* Precious; extremely important or useful. *Ex.* Albert Einstein made invaluable contributions to scientific research. (p. 82)

inventory *n.* A complete list. *Ex.* The department store will be closed tomorrow to do an inventory of everything in the store. (p. 96)

irreversible *adj.* Cannot be changed or turned back. *Ex.* Time is irreversible; you will never get younger! (p. 96)

irritable *adj.* Easily angered or annoyed. *Ex.* People are often irritable if they don't get enough sleep. (p. 107)

jog *v.* To give a little push; to shake. *Ex.* I keep a note on my office door to jog my memory to turn off the coffeepot at the end of the day. (p. 139)

kick off *v.* (informal). To start. *Ex.* The department store will kick off its big sale with free balloons, candy, and door prizes. (p. 24)

lapse *n.* An interval or period of time. *Ex.* When I saw him, there was a time lapse of a few seconds before I remembered his name. (p. 137)

last *v.* To continue; to endure. *Ex.* The party lasted until late at night. (p. 32)

let alone *phrase.* Since the first thing is not true, the second thing can't be either. *Ex.* I can't even float let alone swim. (p. 125)

lift *n.* A good feeling; a rise in spirits. *Ex.* I always get a lift when someone compliments me. (p. 107)

link *v.* To join; to connect. *Ex.* The Panama Canal links the Atlantic Ocean with the Pacific Ocean. (p. 138)

locate *v.* To find something in a particular place. *Ex.* I'm trying to locate Mr. Smith; is his office on this floor? (p. 44)

logical *adj.* Sensible; using good judgment. *Ex.* Martha has a logical reason for studying biology; she wants to be a doctor. (p. 128)

lush *adj.* Very abundant growth. *Ex.* The lush rice fields of Bali spread out as far as the eye can see. (p. 96)

major *adj.* Very important. *Ex.* If I have a major problem I can always talk to my sister. (p. 32)

manners *n. plural.* Polite behavior. *Ex.* In England, it is good manners to stand in line at the bus stop. (p. 74)

marshall up (one's) courage *v.* To become brave. *Ex.* Georgie marshalled up his courage and asked Lydia to marry him. (p. 116)

masculine *adj.* Concerning men; typical of men. *Ex.* Those football players look very strong and masculine. (p. 15)

mass destruction *phrase.* Terrible damage that affects many people. *Ex.* The 1991 typhoon in Bangladesh caused mass destruction to homes and farms, and killed over 100,000 people. (p. 99)

massacre *n.* The killing of many people at one time. *Ex.* The massacre of innocent people in war is always terrible. (p. 97)

matters *n. plural.* Circumstances, events. *Ex.* For legal matters, you should speak to a lawyer. (p. 83)

media *n. plural.* Sources for news, such as radio, TV, newspapers and magazines. *Ex.* The media are always looking for exciting stories. (p. 117)

mentally *adv.* Using your mind; thinking. *Ex.* Ms. Shimada added up the prices mentally and realized she didn't have enough money with her. (p. 146)

metaphor *n.* A description of something by saying it is something else; a symbol for something. *Ex.* In my culture, an ox is a metaphor for strength and endurance. (p. 104)

mill *v.* To make (steel, paper, flour) in a factory. *Ex.* Which country in the world mills the most steel? (p. 23)

miner *n.* A person who works underground to dig things out of the rock (such as coal, silver, diamonds). *Ex.* The miners hoped to find gold in the mountains. (p. 23)

minimize *v.* To make as small as possible. *Ex.* To minimize the chance of illness, be sure to eat well and get enough sleep. (p. 23)

minor *adj.* Small; not important. *Ex.* You did very well on the test; there are just a few minor errors. (p. 128)

minute *adj.* Very small; tiny. *Ex.* Even a minute amount of wine can make me feel dizzy. (p. 45)

minutely *adv.* In great detail. *Ex.* The scientists studied the moon rocks minutely to learn everything about them. (p. 84)

miserable *adj.* Very unhappy. *Ex.* Claude felt miserable when he lost his car keys. (p. 63)

mission *n.* An important duty or job. *Ex.* The astronauts' mission was to conduct experiments in their spaceship. (p. 114)

monitor *v.* To watch closely. *Ex.* The parents monitored their sick child all night. (p. 44)

monologue *n.* A long speech by one person. *Ex.* The actor had difficulty memorizing the long monologue. (p. 115)

mumble *v.* To speak softly and unclearly. *Ex.* Frederick came to the meeting late and mumbled an apology. (p. 84)

my kind *phrase.* Something or someone similar to me; something that I like. *Ex.* A sports car is my kind of car! (p. 115)

mysterious *adj.* Puzzling; impossible to understand. *Ex.* He took some mysterious letters out of his pocket and gave them to the detective. (p. 130)

negative *adj.* Seeing the bad side of something. *Ex.* If children have negative feelings about school, they probably won't do well. (p. 93)

nervous *adj.* Worried; not calm. *Ex.* Mr. Lewis was nervous the first time he flew in an airplane. (p. 32)

neutral *adj.* Plain; without any special color. *Ex.* If you paint the walls a neutral white, you will be able to decorate with any color. (p. 23)

nobility *n.* High character or quality that you admire. *Ex.* We could tell the nobility of her character from the way she spoke to us. (p. 15)

nostalgic *adj.* Full of good memories for things of the past. *Ex.* Mr. Martelli had nostalgic memories of his childhood home in Sicily.

object to *v. phrase.* To oppose; to disagree. *Ex.* I object to your plan because it is too expensive. (p. 3)

obsessed (be obsessed with) *v.* To think about something all the time. *Ex.* Peter became obsessed with learning to play the piano; he practices all the time. (p. 1)

obstruct *v.* To block; to cover. *Ex.* The trees obstruct our view of the lake. (p. 84)

occur *v.* To happen. *Ex.* The final examination will occur on the same day as the class party. (p. 32)

odds see *against all odds.*

ointment *n.* A cream or oil to rub on the skin. *Ex.* This ointment should help your stiff muscles. (p. 15)

oohs and ahs *phrase.* Sounds of praise or appreciation. *Ex.* You will hear lots of oohs and ahs at the circus when performers do difficult tricks. (p. 73)

openers see *for openers.*

oppose *v.* To be against; to disapprove. *Ex.* Do you oppose the new tax or are you for it? (p. 85)

orient *v.* To adjust to; to adapt. *Ex.* When I moved to Chicago, I had difficulty orienting myself to the subway (metro) system. (p. 53)

origin *n.* Beginning; source. *Ex.* Lake Victoria in Africa is the origin of the Nile River. (p. 23)

outlook *n.* Way of thinking; viewpoint. *Ex.* If you have a positive outlook on life, you will be happy. (p. 82)

overalls *n. plural.* Loose pants that you wear over your regular clothes to keep them clean while you are working. *Ex.* The auto mechanic wore overalls. (p. 23)

overture *n.* An offer; an attempt to get to know someone. *Ex.* Shy people are often afraid that people will reject their overture of friendship. (p. 114)

overwhelmed *adj.* Feeling that too many things are happening at the same time. *Ex.* Peter was overwhelmed on the first day of his new job because there were so many things to learn. (p. 87)

panic *v.* To become afraid suddenly. *Ex.* My dog always panics at the sound of thunder. (p. 45)

passive *adj.* Not reacting. *Ex.* Mahatma Gandhi believed in passive resistance as a way to make political change. (p. 107)

paste *n.* A soft, sticky mixture. *Ex.* You can make tomato sauce by mixing tomato paste, water, and some herbs. (p. 15)

pathetic *adj.* Sad and unfortunate. *Ex.* The refugees looked hungry and pathetic as they walked over the mountains. (p. 116)

pattern *n.* A model; a design. *Ex.* Do you prefer a pattern of stripes or circles? (p. 46)

pause *v.* To stop for a short time. *Ex.* On television and radio, the announcer says, "We now pause for station identification." (pp. 85, 148)

persuade *v.* To convince. *Ex.* Can you persuade Ms. Lippe to come to the movies with us? (p. 54)

phenomenal *adj.* Remarkable; very large or great. *Ex.* The play is a phenomenal success; everyone wants to see it. (p. 130)

phenomenon *n.* (phenomena, pl.) A scientific fact or event that you can observe. *Ex.* I think a rainbow is the most beautiful natural phenomenon. (p. 137)

pierce *v.* To cut into something with a sharp object; to make a hole through something. *Ex.* The instructions on the popcorn bag say "Pierce this bag in several places with a fork before placing it in the microwave oven." (p. 148)

play up *v.* To emphasize. *Ex.* Be sure to play up your good points during your job interview. (p. 15)

plead my case *v.* (legal term). To speak in support of someone or something in court. *Ex.* The lawyer pleaded the thief's case so successfully that he got only a short jail sentence. (p. 116)

pool (our) resources *v.* To gather together and share. *Ex.* The farmers pooled their resources and bought some expensive farm equipment that they all could use. (p. 116)

portrait *n.* A picture of a person. *Ex.* Portraits of all the presidents are displayed in that hallway. (p. 105)

possession *n.* Something that belongs to you. *Ex.* I moved all my possessions to my new apartment. (p. 74)

postpone *v.* To delay; to put off. *Ex.* We postponed the picnic because it rained. (p. 96)

potential *adj.* Possible in the future. *Ex.* The doctors discussed the potential uses of the new drug. (p. 116)

precisely *adv.* Exactly. *Ex.* I have precisely enough money to go to the movies. (p. 72)

predict *v.* To look into the future; to anticipate. *Ex.* The weather report predicts that it will rain all week. (p. 34)

preserve *v.* To save; to maintain. *Ex.* It is important to preserve the tropical rain forests. (p. 64)

press one's luck *v.* To take too many chances. *Ex.* Don't press your luck; the dog might bite you if you tease it again. (p. 115)

profusely *adv.* Very much. *Ex.* The runner was sweating profusely by the end of the race. (p. 116)

program oneself *v.* To train oneself. *Ex.* Charles programmed himself to wake up at 6 A.M. every morning. (p. 128)

proposed *adj.* Suggested. *Ex.* Your proposed plan sounds interesting. (p. 96)

proposition *n.* A statement expressing a theory or opinion. *Ex.* The Declaration of Independence makes the proposition that all people are created equal. (p. 104)

prosperous *adj.* Doing well; wealthy and successful. *Ex.* Saudi Arabia is a very prosperous country because of its oil. (p. 117)

proud *adj.* To feel good about something that you have done or are connected to. *Ex.* Sidney is proud of his Polish heritage. (p. 4)

purity *n.* Clean; clear; without any faults. *Ex.* I love the purity of the mountain air. (p. 15)

pursue *v.* To find out more about something by studying it carefully; to go after. *Ex.* The scientists are pursuing the causes of cancer. (p. 104)

put up with *v.* To accept whatever happens; to tolerate. *Ex.* How do you put up with your noisy neighbors? (p. 63)

randomly selected *phrase.* Chosen without any order or plan. *Ex.* The winning numbers in the lottery are randomly selected. (p. 107)

rank *n.* Level; position. *Ex.* She reached the rank of Vice President of the company before she retired. (p. 16)

rarely *adv.* Almost never. *Ex.* Mr. Santos rarely takes a vacation. (p. 105)

react *v.* To respond. *Ex.* How did Mrs. Chernin react when you told her that she won the contest? (p. 45)

recall *v.* To remember. *Ex.* I can't recall his name, but I think it starts with a "G." (p. 125)

regret *v.* To feel sorry about something. *Ex.* I regret that I can't come to your wedding, but I'll be out of town that week. (p. 128)

rehearsal *n.* A practice session. *Ex.* The final rehearsal of the play was yesterday; the show opens tonight. (p. 53)

reign *n.* The time when a king or queen rules a country. *Ex.* The reign of Louis the Fourteenth of France lasted from 1643 to 1715. (p. 15)

reinforce *v.* To make stronger. *Ex.* Every time I visit Buenos Aires, it reinforces my love of Argentina. (p. 129)

relationship *n.* Connection; involvement. *Ex.* I have a close relationship with my grandfather because I lived with him when I was a child. (p. 64)

relative *n.* A member of your family. *Ex.* All my relatives still live in Peru. (p. 74)

relatively *adv.* Comparatively; rather. *Ex.* Vegetables are relatively cheap in California because they are grown there. (p. 74)

relay *v.* To send to another person. *Ex.* Please relay my best regards to your parents. (p. 97)

reliable *adj.* Believable; trustworthy. *Ex.* The information in that newspaper is always reliable; you can believe it. (p. 45)

reluctance *n.* Unwillingness; hesitancy. *Ex.* He ate the strange food with great reluctance. (p. 84)

reluctant *adj.* Hesitant, unwilling. *Ex.* I am reluctant to lend you any more money until you pay back the money I gave you last month. (p. 64)

repair *v.* To fix. *Ex.* Mr. Valmont repairs watches and clocks. (p. 116)

report *v.* To tell the facts. *Ex.* The newspaper reported on the elections. (p. 45)

rerun *n.* Showing a television program or movie again. *Ex.* In the summer, many television stations show reruns of popular programs from the past year.

rescue *v.* To save. *Ex.* The firefighters rescued the children from the burning house. (p. 34)

resist *v.* To stay away from; to oppose. *Ex.* I can't resist chocolate cake; it's my favorite dessert. (p. 65)

resort to *v.* To do something in a certain way in order to achieve something. *Ex.* Ivan finally resorted to sharing an apartment with his brother because he couldn't afford the rent by himself. (p. 114)

restless *adj.* Not relaxed; moving nervously. *Ex.* Ms. Rosen was restless while she waited for the results of the medical tests. (p. 45)

restrain *v.* To hold back; to control. *Ex.* I restrained myself from speaking even though I was very angry. (p. 83)

retain *v.* To keep; to continue to have. *Ex.* I can't retain all that information without taking notes. (p. 148)

retrace *v.* To review; to go over again. *Ex.* To find her lost umbrella, Sheila retraced her day's activities and found it in the restaurant where she ate lunch. (p. 139)

review *v.* To look at something again; to think about again. *Ex.* Before I go to sleep, I like to review all the things that happened to me that day. (p. 130)

reward *v.* To give a prize or payment. *Ex.* That school rewards the best students with scholarships. (p. 72)

rough going *phrase.* Full of problems; difficult. *Ex.* Driving on that narrow mountain road was really rough going! (p. 114)

roughly *adv.* Approximately. *Ex.* I have roughly thirty dollars in my wallet. (p. 14)

rugged *adj.* Strong; rough; forceful. *Ex.* I love the rugged beauty of the mountains. (p. 15)

ruin see *in ruin*.

run wild *v.* To go out of control; to be unrestrained. *Ex.* The poet let her imagination run wild as she wrote her poems. (p. 84)

rural *adj.* Farm and small town. *Ex.* Jan grew up in a rural area of Norway. (p. 99)

rush *v.* To hurry; to go quickly. *Ex.* The ambulance rushed to the hospital. (p. 127)

sake see *for his sake*.

sanction *n.* Approval; consent. *Ex.* Paul got his parents' sanction to go to an expensive college. (p. 82)

scattered *adj.* Spread around in various places. *Ex.* The children left their toys scattered all over the floor. (pp. 96, 149)

scramble *v.* To move in a hurry, sometimes close to the ground. *Ex.* You have to scramble through the bushes to get to the lake. (p. 119)

scrutinize *v.* Examine closely; study. *Ex.* Mr. Sampson scrutinized the painting for a long time before buying it. (p. 83)

sedative *n.* Something that makes you sleepy. *Ex.* If you can't fall asleep, drink some warm milk as a sedative. (p. 106)

seismic *adj.* Concerning an earthquake. (p. 44)

seismograph *n.* Equipment that records earthquake motion. (p. 44)

seize the moment *v.* To take the opportunity. *Ex.* The time was right, so I seized the moment and asked Rachel to marry me. (p. 115)

shave *v.* To cut off with a razor. *Ex.* Paul shaves his face every morning. (p. 2)

shed new light on *v.* To provide new information; to make something easier to understand. *Ex.* That research will shed new light on heart disease. (p. 106)

shook (past tense of *shake*) To move back and forth quickly. *Ex.* The trees shook when the wind blew hard. (p. 32)

shrink *v.* To make smaller. *Ex.* If you wash wool socks in hot water, they will shrink. (p. 23)

signify *v.* To have a particular meaning. *Ex.* The red light signifies "stop," and the green light signifies "go." (p. 15)

singularly *adv.* Unusually. *Ex.* Ms. Elkins is singularly fond of California wines. (p. 114)

sip *n.* A little taste of a liquid. *Ex.* She took two sips of the wine and said it was delicious. (p. 84)

slight *adj.* Very small. *Ex.* There is a slight chance of rain today. (p. 149)

slyly *adv.* Done in a clever way, possibly to embarrass someone. *Ex.* He remarked slyly that he had seen them in the park (when they were supposed to be at work). (p. 15)

snapshot *n.* A photograph. *Ex.* My mother keeps all the family snapshots in a big box. (pp. 117, 147)

sniff *n.* and *v.* Taking a quick, short breath through the nose. *Ex.* The cat sniffed the food before eating it.

snug *adj.* Tight. *Ex.* My clothes feel snug; I must have gained some weight. (p. 23)

soak *v.* To leave in water for a while. *Ex.* Soak the dried mushrooms in water until they are soft, and then cook them. (p. 23)

soil *n.* Dirt. *Ex.* Gina planted her tomato plants in rich soil in her garden. (p. 23)

sole *adj.* The only one. *Ex.* My aunt is the sole owner of that bookstore. (p. 114)

speculation *n.* A guess. *Ex.* Is it speculation or a fact that it will snow tomorrow? (p. 85)

spook *v.* To frighten. *Ex.* Children enjoy spooking adults on Halloween. (p. 136)

spreadsheet *n.* A page of an accounting report. *Ex.* The Accounting Department prepares spreadsheets to show how much money is spent each month on salaries, travel, and office expenses. (p. 96)

stain *n.* A dirty spot. *Ex.* I can't get these ink stains off my shirt. (p. 23)

stare *v.* To look at directly; to keep one's eyes on. *Ex.* He stared at the painting for a long time. (pp. 53, 85)

state-of-the-art *phrase.* Most current; up-to-date. *Ex.* State-of-the-art computers are very powerful. (p. 95)

status *n.* A level in a group. *Ex.* Teachers and doctors have a high status in Korea. (p. 16)

steep *adj.* Tilted at a very great angle. *Ex.* Switzerland is famous for its steep mountains. (p. 52)

stiff *adj.* Not bending; not flexible. *Ex.* The stiff leather shoes hurt my feet. (p. 23)

stimulate *v.* To encourage; to cause a sudden increase in activity. *Ex.* The smell of the roast chicken stimulated my appetite, and I said "Let's eat!" (p. 148)

stir up *v.* To awaken; to begin to think about something. *Ex.* When I visit my children's school, it stirs up memories of my own school days.

stitch *v.* To sew. *Ex.* Let me stitch up that torn pocket. (p. 23)

storage *n.* Keeping something for the future. *Ex.* Put the extra furniture in storage while you decide what to do with it. (p. 125)

strategy *n.* A careful plan. *Ex.* Mr. Neilsen has developed a strategy for expanding his real estate business. (p. 125)

strictly *adv.* Completely; only. *Ex.* I am strictly a vegetarian, so I don't eat any meat or fish. (p. 24)

struggle *v.* To fight; to have difficulty doing something. *Ex.* In the monster movie, the dinosaur struggled with the giant gorilla. (p. 52)

suave *adj.* Charming and polite. *Ex.* The movie star always looked very suave and elegant. (p. 116)

subjects see *control subjects.*

successive *adj.* One after another without any interruption. *Ex.* My family has lived in this house for five successive generations. (p. 147)

supplies *n. plural.* Items to be kept and used as needed. *Ex.* The mountain climbers took all their supplies with them. (p. 34)

survivor *n.* One who remains alive. *Ex.* There were three survivors of the car accident. (p. 32)

susceptible to *adj.* Easily affected by something. *Ex.* I am very susceptible to colds and the flu every winter.

sway *v.* To move back and forth. *Ex.* The trees swayed in the strong wind. (p. 32)

tactic *n.* Method to achieve a particular goal. *Ex.* What tactics should I use to get a job? (p. 114)

tailor *n.* A person who sews or makes clothing. *Ex.* The tailor fixed the sleeves on my jacket. (p. 23)

take in *v.* To see; to observe closely. *Ex.* The festival was so big that I couldn't take in all the events. (p. 85)

technology *n.* The combination of scientific knowledge and methods. *Ex.* Medical technology can identify all kinds of medical problems. (p. 93)

tell X from Y *v.* To recognize the difference; to distinguish one thing from another. *Ex.* Look at these two paintings; can you tell the original from the copy? (p. 5)

tend *v.* To move in a certain direction; to choose. *Ex.* Jane tends to take her vacations in Florida because she likes warm weather. (p. 46)

terror *n.* Great fear. *Ex.* Snakes and spiders fill some people with terror. (p. 32)

textile *n.* Cloth; fabric. *Ex.* The silk textiles from Thailand are very beautiful. (p. 23)

theorize *v.* To develop a theory or idea. *Ex.* Astronomers theorize that there could be life on other planets. (p. 137)

tingle *v.* To feel a prickling sensation. *Ex.* My leg began to tingle after I had sat in one position for a long time.

tip *n.* 1. small amount of money in payment for a service. *Ex.* Give the taxi driver a ten percent tip. (p. 72) 2. The very end; the point. *Ex.* You could see the tip of the mountain appearing above the clouds. (p. 84)

tool *n.* Something that helps you do a job. *Ex.* Hammers and saws are tools used by carpenters. (p. 97)

trace *n.* A very small amount. *Ex.* You can see traces of snow on the mountain-top even in summer. (p. 115)

track *n.* (keep on track) A path; a direction; something that leads to a goal. *Ex.* By studying English and learning computer programming, you are on the right track for a good job.

transfer *v.* To move from one position to another. *Ex.* Michael transferred some money from his savings account to a checking account. (p. 84)

treasure *v.* To appreciate greatly; to prize. *Ex.* Ms. Kim treasures the memories of her vacation in Paris. (p. 64)

tremendous *adj.* Very large. *Ex.* There was a tremendous wedding cake for the 400 guests. (p. 44)

tribal *adj.* Belonging to a united group. *Ex.* The tribal customs of American Indian nations vary from tribe to tribe. (p. 53)

troop *n.* An organized group (ex: soldiers, scouts). *Ex.* I belonged to a Girl Scout troop in junior high school. (p. 97)

trough *n.* A long narrow box for feeding animals or giving them water. *Ex.* The cows come to the trough to eat the hay. (p. 23)

trousers *n.* plural. Long pants. *Ex.* A suit is made up of a jacket and trousers. (p. 23)

tuck away *v.* To put away safely. *Ex.* Every month I tuck away some money for my vacation. (p. 117)

turn the tables on *v.* To make something happen the opposite of how it was originally planned. *Ex.* John wanted to borrow money from me, but I turned the tables on him and asked to borrow money from him first!

twilight zone *phrase.* An unclear situation in which nothing seems normal. *Ex.* Many science fiction stories take place in a twilight zone where the hero thinks he is going crazy because strange things happen. (p. 115)

unharmed *adj.* Not damaged; not hurt. *Ex.* The cat jumped off the roof and landed unharmed on its feet. (p. 35)

unstable *adj.* Weak; not solid. *Ex.* That old chair is very unstable; don't sit on it. (p. 35)

unsuitable *adj.* Not appropriate. *Ex.* It is unsuitable to wear a business suit and tie to the beach. (p. 73)

upcoming *adj.* Happening soon. *Ex.* Every Friday, the newspaper has information on upcoming sports events. (p. 43)

vanish *v.* To disappear. *Ex.* The magician made the birds vanish right before our eyes. (p. 116)

vanity *n.* A great amount of pride in oneself. *Ex.* He dyed his hair because of his vanity about his appearance. (p. 14)

videotape *v.* To film onto magnetic tape. *Ex.* The Hansens videotaped their son's wedding. (p. 96)

virtually *adv.* Almost entirely. *Ex.* When I arrived in Toronto, I knew virtually no one, but now I have lots of friends. (p. 72)

vision *n.* A dream; an image. *Ex.* The philosopher described her vision of the future. (p. 85)

visualize *v.* To form a picture in your mind. *Ex.* I've read that there are billions of stars in the universe, but I can't really visualize what "a billion" is. (p. 146)

vivid *adj.* Strong; bright; described clearly. *Ex.* My grandmother told vivid stories of her life on a farm in the early 1900s. (p. 147)

warning *n.* Notification before danger or a problem. *Ex.* The flashing red lights are a warning that a train is coming. (p. 46)

weapon *n.* Something to fight with; something that can injure. *Ex.* The detective said, "Drop your weapon and put your hands up." (p. 99)

weird *adj.* Very strange. *Ex.* Don't you think that some modern music sounds weird? (pp. 16, 53)

wild see *run wild*.

with ease *phrase.* Easily. *Ex.* A good swimmer can swim a quarter mile (half a kilometer) with ease. (p. 125)

wizard *n.* A person with unusual skills or abilities. *Ex.* Steve is a wizard with computers. (p. 130)

wonders see *do wonders*.

worth (be worth) *v.* To have value. *Ex.* My car is worth about $7000. (p. 96)

would-be *phrase.* Future; want to be. *Ex.* The would-be opera singer took voice lessons for many years. (p. 114)

wrapping *n.* A covering (often of paper or plastic). *Ex.* Take the wrapping off the present so we can see what it is. (p. 74)

CREDITS

Photo Credits

pp. x, 2, 12, 22, 26, 43, 71, 97, 113, 115, 118, 124, 134, 139, 145, 147
Michael O. Lajoie

p. 14   Comstock, Inc./George Gerster
p. 26   The Bettmann Archive
p. 30   Reuters/Bettmann
p. 33   UPI/Bettmann
p. 45   Bill Grant–Staff/The Christian Science Monitor
p. 50   Reuters/Bettmann
p. 55   UPI/Bettmann
p. 60   (*top*) Richard Lucas/The Image Works
p. 60   (*bottom*) Courtesy of Madavi Rajguru
p. 73   Courtesy of Louise Hirasawa
p. 79   Mark Antman/The Image Works
p. 83   Antoinette Jongen/FPG International
p. 92   Reuters/Bettmann
p. 94   Lionel Delevingne/Stock, Boston
p. 105 Dorien Grunbaum
p. 134 Courtesy of Louise Hirasawa

Text/Realia Credits

p. 23   Excerpt from EXTRAORDINARY ORIGINS OF EVERYDAY THINGS, by Charles Panati. Copyright © 1987 by Charles Panati. Reprinted by permission of HarperCollins Publishers.
p. 35   *Newsweek*, December 8, 1980
pp. 41, 42 *The World Almanac & Book of Facts*, 1991 edition, copyright Pharos Books 1990, New York, NY 10166.
p. 51   "In a Collapsed Building...", Katherine Bishop, *The New York Times*, October 19, 1989
p. 52   "Not in City for Quake...", *The New York Times*, October 23, 1989
p. 62   "Dear Abby" by Abigail Van Buren, © 1992 Universal Press Syndicate. Reprinted with permission. All rights reserved.
p. 63   "Dear Abby" by Abigail Van Buren, © 1991 Universal Press Syndicate. Reprinted with permission. All rights reserved.
pp. 69–70 Copyright © 1985 by Houghton Mifflin Company. Reprinted by permission from THE AMERICAN HERITAGE DICTIONARY, SECOND COLLEGE EDITION.
p. 72   "Verboten in One Place, de Riguer in Another" by Stanley Carr, *New York Times* Travel Section, March 11, 1984
p. 82   From THE VENDOR OF SWEETS by R.K. Narayan, Copyright © 1958, renewed 1986 by R.K. Narayan. Reprinted by permission of Viking Penguin, a division of Penguin Books USA Inc. Reprinted by permission of Wallace Literary Agency, Inc.